CREASE-CRASHING
HOCKEY
TRIVIA

GREY*S*TONE BOOKS
Douglas & McIntyre Publishing Group
Vancouver/Toronto/Berkeley

To Gump Worsley, the reigning rubber king, with 352 glorious losses.

Greystone Books
A division of Douglas & McIntyre Ltd.
2323 Quebec Street, Suite 201
Vancouver, British Columbia
Canada v5t 4s7
www.greystonebooks.com

Library and Archives Canada Cataloguing in Publication
Weekes Don
        Crease-crashing hockey trivia / Don Weekes
ISBN: 978-1-55365-328-8

      1. National Hockey League—Miscellanea 2. Hockey—Miscellanea.
I. Title.

GV847.8.N3W4185 2007   796.962'64   C2007-902951-5

Editing by Anne Rose
Cover and text design by Lisa Hemingway
Cover photo © Bruce Bennett / Getty Images
Printed and bound in Canada by Friesens
Distributed in the U.S. by Publishers Group West

We gratefully acknowledge the financial support of the Canada Council for the Arts,
the British Columbia Arts Council, the Province of British Columbia through the Book
Publishing Tax Credit, and the Government of Canada through the Book Publishing
Industry Development Program (BPIDP) for our publishing activities.

DON WEEKES *is an award-winning television producer at* CTV *in Montreal. He has written
numerous hockey trivia books, including co-authoring the* Unofficial Guide *series.*

Contents

1

Rally Cry

AFTER TRAILING **WASHINGTON 4–0** in a December 2006 game featuring puck prodigies Sidney Crosby and Alex Ovechkin, Pittsburgh rallied with four unanswered goals in a wild comeback courtesy of youngsters Maxine Talbot, Erik Christensen, Crosby and Evgeni Malkin. No scoring in overtime brought out the snipers, and a new trick in the shootout. On the bench, the entire Penguin team wore their helmets backward—rally style. The helmet move paid off, with Marc-Andre Fleury turning aside every shooter except Ovechkin. Meanwhile, Olaf Kolzig gave up goals to Christensen and Malkin, who slipped a beautiful backhand past the Capitals goalie while sprawled chest-first in front of the net. "Nothing is a lock, you know," confessed Ovechkin after the 5–4 loss.

Answers are on page 7

1.1 **What is a cap trick?**
   A. A practical joke played on rookies
   B. Two goals in regulation time and one in the shootout
   C. A helmet modification that provides greater ventilation
   D. A CBA loophole for salary-cap relief

1.2 **Why does Sidney Crosby wear No. 87?**

A. No. 87 represents his birthdate

B. No. 87 is the number his father wore

C. No. 87 is the only number that no other NHL player has worn

D. No. 87 matches the number of goals he scored in peewee hockey

1.3 **In 2006, who set a new record for the hardest shot ever recorded?**

A. Sami Salo of the Vancouver Canucks

B. Jarome Iginla of the Calgary Flames

C. Chad Kilger of the Toronto Maple Leafs

D. Sheldon Souray of the Montreal Canadiens

1.4 **Which NHL defenseman became the new ironman among blueliners in 2006–07?**

A. Cory Sarich of the Tampa Bay Lightning

B. Mathieu Dandenault of the Montreal Canadiens

C. Karlis Skrastins of the Colorado Avalanche

D. Chris Chelios of the Detroit Red Wings

1.5 **The late broadcaster Danny Gallivan coined the term "spin-o-rama" (or "spinnerama") to describe a deke first used by which NHLer?**

A. Serve Savard of the Montreal Canadiens

B. Denis Savard of the Chicago Blackhawks

C. Andre Savard of the Buffalo Sabres

D. None of the above; Danny Gallivan used "swirl-a-rama"

1.6　What is the unofficial NHL record for ice time in a game by a player who registered a Gordie Howe hat trick—a goal, an assist and a fight?

A. Under five minutes

B. Between five and 10 minutes

C. One period

D. Two periods

1.7　Who is Rip Simonick?

A. An alias for NHL free agents

B. The Buffalo Sabres' equipment manager

C. A statistician with the CBC's *Hockey Night in Canada*

D. An IIHF official who criticized the NHL for raiding European leagues

1.8　On March 3, 1968, which arena hosted the only double-header in NHL history?

A. Boston Garden

B. The Montreal Forum

C. Chicago Stadium

D. Madison Square Garden

1.9　What inspired San Jose forward Jonathan Cheechoo, when he was 12 years old, to predict that he would play with the Sharks?

A. A Sharks team jacket

B. A rare shark attack in Hudson Bay

C. A fishing trip off the coast of California

D. The 1970s hit song "Do You Know the Way to San Jose?"

1.10 At the start of 2006–07, Los Angeles GM Dean Lombardi made a bet with Kings forward Alexander Frolov, agreeing that if Frolov "showed more determination with the puck," he would read which Russian novel?

A. *Doctor Zhivago*

B. *The Brothers Karamazov*

C. *War and Peace*

D. *A Hero of Our Time*

1.11 In January 2006, how long were the pregame retirement ceremonies honouring Steve Yzerman?

A. About 15 minutes

B. Between 15 and 45 minutes

C. Between 45 and 75 minutes

D. About 90 minutes

1.12 Who was the only player to captain Steve Yzerman in NHL play?

A. Dale McCourt

B. Danny Gare

C. Reed Larson

D. Detroit had no full captain until Steve Yzerman

1.13 In December 2006, a high-profile charity game featuring hockey greats was played in Moscow's Red Square. What was the age of the youngest player who participated in that old-timers match?

A. 10 years old

B. 20 years old

C. 30 years old

D. 40 years old

1.14 In a January 2007 Edmonton–Dallas game, which Stars player skated in alone with the Oilers' net empty for the extra attacker, tried to shoot but missed the net, then fell and lost the puck—only to have Edmonton storm back and score to tie the game with two seconds remaining?

A. Mike Ribeiro

B. Jere Lehtinen

C. Stu Barnes

D. Patrik Stefan

1.15 Journeyman winger Bates Battaglia's grandfather, Sam Battaglia, was famous for running a business in what line of work?

A. Medicine

B. Crime

C. Entertainment

D. Agriculture

1.16 Who is Arthur Farrell?

A. A well-known shot-blocking coach for defensemen

B. The designer of the NHL's new uniforms

C. The author of the first book written about hockey

D. The first non-NHLer inducted into the Hockey Hall of Fame

1.17 Responding to a reporter, Minnesota Wild coach Jacques Lemaire once said: "No? Really? That's why I'm so tired. That's definitely why I'm so tired." Why was Lemaire "tired"?

A. He held the longest practice in team history

B. His Wild set a league record for longest road trip

C. His Wild played back-to-back games in less than 24 hours

D. He had coached his 1,000th career game

1.18 **Who is nicknamed Captain Canada?**

A. Joe Sakic

B. Ryan Smyth

C. Scott Niedermayer

D. Steve Yzerman

1.19 **Who owns the puck with which Maurice Richard scored his 325th NHL goal on November 8, 1952, to break Nels Stewart's all-time record?**

A. His brother, Henri

B. Queen Elizabeth II

C. The Hockey Hall of Fame

D. The Canadian Museum of Civilization

1.20 **Which NHL tough guy played the role of New York Rangers enforcer Bob "Killer" Dill in the 2006 film about Maurice Richard, *The Rocket*?**

A. Sean Avery

B. Andre Roy

C. Colton Orr

D. Brian McGrattan

1.21 **The average number of goals scored per game in the NHL rose from 5.1 to 6.1 in 2005–06. How many years has it been since the league had a season with a larger increase?**

A. 20 years

B. 35 years

C. 50 years

D. 75 years

1.22 **What finally forced Joe Nieuwendyk to quit hockey in mid-2006–07?**

A. Tendonitis in the elbow

B. A rotator cuff problem

C. Chronic back pain

D. Severe ACL damage in his right knee

1.23 **Who amassed the most points per minutes played in 2006–07?**

A. Sidney Crosby of the Pittsburgh Penguins

B. Joe Thornton of the San Jose Sharks

C. Teemu Selanne of the Anaheim Ducks

D. Jason Spezza of the Ottawa Senators

Rally Cry

Answers

1.1 **B. Two goals in regulation time and one in the shootout**

Since shootout goals don't officially count in a player's scoring totals, it's not called a hat trick when the third goal comes in the shootout. In hockey jargon, it's sometimes called a cap trick.

1.2 **A. No. 87 represents his birthdate**

Several NHL stars have selected unconventional uniform numbers. Mario Lemieux chose No. 66 because it was the reverse of Wayne Gretzky's 99. Jaromir Jagr picked No. 68 because it represented the year of the Prague Spring, 1968's short-lived surge of social reform in his home country of Czechoslovakia. In Sidney Crosby's case, the motivation is numerical symbolism. The Penguins phenom wears No. 87 because it represents the year, month and day of his birth: August 7, 1987.

1.3 C. Chad Kilger of the Toronto Maple Leafs

On December 3, 2006, Chad Kilger unleashed a 106.6-m.p.h. slap shot at the Toronto Maple Leafs skills competition, setting the unofficial hockey record for hardest shot. Kilger's howitzer broke the old mark of 106.0 m.p.h. held by San Jose's Shawn Heins. The former NHL mark was set by Al Iafrate, who blasted a shot of 105.2 m.p.h. at 1993's NHL All-Star skills competition. Yet despite the velocity he can generate, Kilger has never been much of a scoring threat. The winger has only netted plus-15 goal seasons twice in his 11-year NHL career. Asked by reporters why he doesn't score more with his blistering shot, Kilger replied: "The defenses these days are all so good, and you don't have that many chances or that much time to take a shot."

1.4 C. Karlis Skrastins of the Colorado Avalanche

When this endurance record was smashed, many hockey fans had the same reaction: A blank stare followed by the inevitable, Karlis who? Fair enough. Among the game's ironmen, only a handful of names resonate with fans. Doug Jarvis and Tim Horton, sure. But Karlis Skrastins? Skrastins must be hockey's least known ironman—or he was until February 8, 2007, when he broke Horton's 486-game durability mark for defensemen in his 487th consecutive match, a 6–3 loss to the Atlanta Thrashers. "He's as under-the-radar as any guy I've ever been around," Colorado coach Joel Quenneville confirmed in a *Canadian Press* story. "He's one guy that really doesn't want attention, doesn't want accolades." Skrastins's

near-anonymous streak began on February 21, 2000, and
ended on February 24, 2007, a remarkable seven-year stretch
that saw him play through several injuries before a bad knee
forced him out on February 25. The 32-year-old rearguard had
appeared in 495 straight games. "If I can be sure I can play
the game I usually play when I'm healthy, I'm going to play,
because pain is part of our game," Skrastins once said about
playing injured. (Ironically, he was nicknamed Scratch by his
teammates, a play on his last name.) Horton's streak lasted
from February 11, 1961, to February 4, 1968. Jarvis holds the
overall record of 964 consecutive games during 13 seasons,
1975–76 to 1987–88.

1.5 A. Serve Savard of the Montreal Canadiens

While Denis Savard (and earlier, Bobby Orr) is more closely
associated with the spin-o-rama, that shifty, on-the-fly
360-degree pivot to maintain puck possession against defensemen, it was Serge Savard whose original move to evade
attacking forwards inspired the late CBC broadcaster Danny
Gallivan to announce, "…Savard avoids Clarke (Bobby) with a
deft spinnerama move…" Later, Denis Savard, tried the tech-
nique, but only when he got to the NHL. "It started off with
me just turning my back to the defenseman to keep the puck
away," Savard told the *Hockey News.* "Then I thought about it,
and said, 'Hey, this could be a pretty good move.' So I prac-
tised it and perfected it."

1.6 A. Under five minutes

Gordie Howe, hockey's greatest all-round player, was capable
of scoring a goal, assisting on another and getting into a
fight—and winning it—on any given night during his 1,767-
game NHL career. And though there is no proof that it has

been done in less ice time, Georges Laraque deserves credit for his Gordie Howe hat trick on November 4, 2006, when he scored on Los Angeles goalie Mathieu Garon, assisted on Ed Jovanovski's goal and beat up Raitis Ivanans in just 4:46 of ice time. Laraque, who was miked for the game, cordially said to Ivanans at the faceoff: "Ya wanna do it? Good luck, then."

1.7   **B. The Buffalo Sabres' equipment manager**

Rip Simonick is the longest-serving equipment manager in the NHL. In fact, he has been with Buffalo since the club entered the league in 1969. Simonick developed a passion for team sports as a 10-year-old, doing odd jobs around Buffalo Memorial Stadium. But after playing Junior B and college, he gave up his dream of playing in the big leagues and settled into repairing gear and sharpening skates with the Sabres organization. "Today, we're labourers, psychologists and baby-sitters. They call me a father figure, because I can do it all," Simonick once told the *Gazette*. Now 57, Simonick has worked with six Buffalo GMs, 15 coaches and 18 captains, but the biggest changes he has noticed after almost 40 years in the game, he says, are bottled water and glove-dryers.

1.8   **D. Madison Square Garden**

After the roof of the Philadelphia Spectrum blew off in a howl-ing snowstorm in 1968, the Flyers were forced to play several "home" games at out-of-town arenas while repairs were made on the building. They played at the Colisée in Quebec City and at Toronto's Maple Leaf Gardens, and, on March 3, the Garden became the only NHL arena to host a doubleheader when Philadelphia battled the Oakland Seals to a 1–1 tie in an after-noon game. Afterwards, in the regularly scheduled nightcap, the hometown Rangers downed Chicago 4–0.

1.9   A. A Sharks team jacket

How does a member of the Moose Cree First Nation pick the
San Jose Sharks as his dream team? Growing up in the remote
Ontario outpost of Moose Factory on James Bay is about as
far as anyone can get from the bright lights of San Jose. Those
wanting to travel to, or beyond, the remote settlement must
endure a trek by boat, snowmobile—*and* truck or helicopter,
depending on the time of year. But then few things are typical in this northern Canadian community. For the young
Cheechoo, watching *Hockey Night in Canada* on television
meant a ride by sled to his grandfather's house; and, without
indoor ice facilities, backyards were the community's standard in rinks. Yet Cheechoo's dream began the day his uncle
sent him a Sharks team jacket with those distinctive teal,
silver and white colours—a sign of things to come. In a subse-
quent school assignment, Cheechoo predicted he would one
day play for his favourite NHL team in San Jose. Sure enough,
10 years later, Cheechoo was living his boyhood fantasy when
he stepped on the ice at the Shark Tank—almost 4,000 miles
away from his Cree home of Moose Factory.

1.10   C. *War and Peace*

Russian literature and hockey are not often mentioned in the
same sentence, but both subjects figured prominently in a
wager made between Los Angeles' Alexander Frolov and Dean
Lombardi. Before the start of 2006–07, Lombardi was trying
to convince Frolov to play with more focus and resolve, when
the Russian forward mentioned he had read Leo Tolstoy's *War
and Peace*—not once, but twice. Given that the novel contains
more than half a million words, this was no small boast.
So Lombardi said he would read the gigantic book if Frolov
showed more on-ice perseverance. The wager seemed to

motivate Frolov, who subsequently led the Kings with a career-best 35 goals and 71 points. (No word yet on how Lombardi likes Tolstoy.)

1.11 D. About 90 minutes

Detroit owner Mike Ilitch may be Hockeytown's greatest fan, but when it comes to team celebrations he is the master of overkill. The guy who got no less than nine family members on the Stanley Cup in 1997, and set a record for more names engraved on the Cup than any other champion, raised the bar with the party he staged for Steve Yzerman on January 2, 2007, when the player's No.19 was hung at Joe Louis Arena. Few people uttered anything but praise, however, until six weeks later at the league's GM meetings when the NHL introduced limits on the length of pregame ceremonies. Yet if any player deserved such a celebration it was Yzerman—Detroit's distinguished leader and the NHL's longest-serving captain. The sold-out crowd was thrilled and stood for numerous ovations during the bash, which featured a mammoth seating arrangement at centre ice to accommodate the more than 40 guests, 27 of whom were introduced one by one before Yzerman took to the podium for his final farewell. By the time it was all over, the puck didn't drop until 8:34 PM Eastern Standard Time, more than 90 minutes after the scheduled 7 PM start time. Yzerman's fête was also a huge TV draw in Canada, with double the numbers of the game that followed: 916,000 viewers when Yzerman spoke and his jersey was raised compared to 400,000 for the 2–1 win against Anaheim.

1.12 B. Danny Gare

In the first three years of Steve Yzerman's 22-year NHL career with Detroit, Danny Gare was team captain. Gare got the "C" in his first full season with the Red Wings in 1982–83, the year before Yzerman joined the club as a rookie. When Gare was traded four years later, Yzerman assumed the captaincy, a post he held for 19 years, until his final season of 2005–06.

1.13   A. 10 years old

To celebrate three Russian milestones (the 60th anniversary of the birth of Russian hockey, the 50th anniversary of the former Soviet Union's first Olympic gold medal in hockey and the 25th anniversary of the famous KLM Line in the 1980s), a charity game between former Soviet greats and old NHLers was played for the first time ever in Moscow's Red Square. An outdoor rink with seating for 2,000 fans was built for the event just a slap shot from Lenin's Tomb, the onion-domed Saint Basil's Cathedral and Spassky Tower, while Scotty Bowman coached Team World, made up of NHL stars such as Jari Kurri, Paul Coffey and Peter Stastny and several Soviet greats, including the Great Five of Soviet hockey: Igor Larionov, Sergei Makarov, Vladimir Krutov and defensemen Vyacheslav Fetisov and Alexei Kasatonov. Midway through the game of three 15-minute periods, Maxim Tretiak, the 10-year-old grandson of legendary netminder Vladislav Tretiak, stepped between the pipes and played six shutout minutes against Team World. The historic event ended in a 10–10 draw.

1.14   D. Patrik Stefan

If you're looking for a highlight play of 2006–07, this might be it. After squandering its 4–1 lead, Edmonton pulled goalie Dwayne Roloson for the extra attacker late in the third period while behind 5–4 to Dallas. The Oilers began their rush, but last-man-back Marc-Andre Bergeron fanned on a pass at the blueline—and Patrik Stefan was there, picked up the loose puck and waltzed in on the empty net to put the game away. The Dallas sniper had so much time, he carried the puck all the way to the net, but lost control of it when it hit bad ice on his backhand. Stefan then fell, giving up the puck to the Oilers, who raced back with time running out and scored when Alex Hemsky banged it past Marty Turco at 19:58 to shock the Stars and force overtime. Rexall Place erupted in pandemonium. The game was tied 5–5. In the shootout, Dallas preserved the win and, luckily, some of its dignity. "They may show it a million times for years to come," said Stefan.

1.15   B. Crime

The real life story of Sam "Teets" Battaglia is like a Mario Puzo novel, or, maybe, an episode of TV's blockbuster hit *The Sopranos.* In fact, Puzo likely found inspiration for *The Godfather* and his popular trilogy of highly acclaimed movies in Mafia bosses such as Battaglia, the notorious don of the Chicago Outfit—the same crime empire that made Al Capone and Sam Giancana household names for their gambling, burglary and loansharking. As a goodfella, Sam Battaglia was arrested 25 times before he was finally jailed for extortion in 1967. He was released from prison and died of cancer in 1973, two years before Bates Battaglia was born. Interestingly, Bates found out about his grandfather's connections to the mob from friends, while playing street hockey.

1.16   C. The author of the first book written about hockey

Hockey: Canada's Royal Winter Game is the oldest surviving book about hockey. And it was written not by a seasoned author or member of the press, but by Arthur Farrell, a hockey player who penned the 122-page read in 1899, the year he won one of two Stanley Cups with the Montreal Shamrocks of the

Amateur Hockey Association of Canada. Farrell's passion for "our glorious sport" offers a rare glimpse into the game in its infancy. "Hockey thrills the player and fascinates the spectator. The swift race up and down the ice, the dodging, the quick passing and fast skating make it an infatuating game." Only a few print editions of Farrell's book are known to exist, but digital copies can be found online.

1.17 D. He had coached his 1,000th career game

Jacques Lemaire is one of the very few NHL coaches with long-term experience who have never been fired. He quit Montreal's bench after 97 games, plagued by the media locust swarm; resigned from New Jersey with 378 games and a Stanley Cup; and, currently, mentors in Minnesota, where he coached his 1,000th career game, a 3–2 win against Los Angeles, on November 11, 2006. The self-deprecating Lemaire, well known for his attention to detail, appeared oblivious to his milestone match—either that or he was just toying with the press when he said, "That's why I'm so tired." At the 1,000-game mark, his record stood at 423–348–129.

1.18 B. Ryan Smyth

It's like the nickname of a 1950s pulp novel or comic book character: Captain Canada. But Ryan Smyth earned the Boy-Scout-like title not for any superhero feats of fiction, but for leading his country to victory on international ice. Since 1995, when he won gold at the World Juniors, Smyth has played 85 games internationally, more than any other Canadian NHLer. He also captained Team Canada for five straight years between 2001 and 2005 at the World Championships, bringing home three gold medals and a silver, and wore Olympic gold on his chest in 2002. "You have to understand," Smyth once told the *Toronto Sun,* "I've played for my country before, and there is nothing better than standing out there hearing that national anthem being played. Nothing." No, Captain Canada doesn't leap tall buildings or save pretty blondes on runaway trains, but he has earned 20 goals, 43 points and 38 penalty minutes in his battle for hockey supremacy.

1.19   B. Queen Elizabeth II

Who would have guessed? The puck that Maurice Richard scored his 325th goal with to break Nels Stewart's all-time NHL record on November 8, 1952, is owned by Queen Elizabeth II. The inscribed, gold-plated puck was presented to the Queen in 1955 by the Montreal Canadiens, evidently because she had expressed an interest in Richard's career after watching him play—in person—at the Montreal Forum during the 1951–52 season.

1.20   A. Sean Avery

Several NHL players had small roles in the 2006 biopic *The Rocket,* about Maurice Richard, including Mike Ricci as Elmer Lach, Vincent Lecavalier as Jean Béliveau and Ian Laperriere as Bernie Geoffrion. But its most memorable cameo belonged to Sean Avery, who played New York Rangers bruiser Bob "Killer" Dill. In the film, Dill is called up from the minors by the Rangers for the sole purpose of goading Richard into a fight, only to be pummelled twice by the Montreal star. Yet, though the movie was faithful to the facts in most respects, this incident was dramatized. Dill tangled twice with Richard during a December 17, 1944, game—once on the ice and then again in the penalty box—and was flattened by Richard in both exchanges, but he was not brought up to the NHL by the Rangers solely for this purpose. In fact, Montreal traded Dill to the Rangers midway through the previous season, and he played nine games against the Canadiens without tangling with Richard before their famous bout in December 1944.

1.21   D. 75 years

The rule changes introduced by the NHL to boost offense after the lockout wiped out the 2004–05 season proved a smashing success. Teams scored a total of 7,443 goals in 2005–06, an average of 6.1 per game and an 18 per cent increase over the average of 5.1 goals scored in 2003–04. The rise marked the largest percentage-increase in goal scoring since 1929–30, when the goals-per-game average jumped from 2.9 to 5.9 thanks to a new rule that permitted forward passing inside all three zones. The boost in overall goal scoring was reflected in substantial point total increases by numerous players, including Carolina's Eric Staal, who posted the biggest jump of 69 points. All told, five players recorded 50 goals, the most since eight players reached the mark in 1995–96.

1.22   C. Chronic back pain

Joe Nieuwendyk had a history of going against his doctors' decisions. And he proved them wrong on more than a few occasions as he matured into a 500-goal scorer with three different Stanley Cup-winning teams in a 20-year span. But when the 40-year-old veteran couldn't get through 60 minutes of hockey for the fourth time in 2006–07, he consulted a back specialist and, this time, followed orders. "I've reached a stage where, structurally, my back isn't going to get any better. So I've decided I'm going to adhere to his [the doctor's] advice this time," said Nieuwendyk in December 2006. Still, Nieuwendyk remained a productive player throughout his career. He had a knack for scoring key goals and winning faceoffs. More precisely, his great outside speed and hand-eye co-ordination won him league-wide respect among his generation, and the Dallas Stars thought so highly of his leadership skills that they even gave up a young prospect named Jarome Iginla to acquire Nieuwendyk from Calgary. Of course, Iginla became the Flames' franchise player, but Nieuwendyk led the Stars with a Conn Smythe-winning performance in 1999's Stanley Cup; "...very classy, unbelievably skilled and clutch," concluded Brett Hull. Nieuwendyk finished his career with 564 goals and 1,126 points in 1,257 games.

1.23 A. Sidney Crosby of the Pittsburgh Penguins

The brave new world of hockey statistics has confirmed what was so evident from the NHL's raw data of 2006–07. Sid the Kid owned the game in his sophomore year. He not only amassed 120 points to win the NHL scoring title, but, based on a more objective statistical analysis called offensive production (which measures scoring per minute of ice time), Crosby also delivered the most offense by cranking out a point every 13.7 minutes while on-ice. Other top guns all ranked high, but on a per-minute basis, Buffalo's Maxim Afinogenov ranked fifth overall with a point every 15.7 minutes of ice time, though he finished 71st in the scoring race.

Moments in Time

SOME HOCKEY DATES are more special than others. For example, if you ask Minnesota backup Josh Harding, he would likely say April 4, 2006, when he became the first netminder to play his first NHL game and record his first win in a shootout. Think you know your hockey history? Really? Match the 10 dates with the corresponding accomplishments, below.

Solutions are on page 120

March 18, 1945   November 1, 1959   February 22, 1980
June 27, 1972   February 7, 1976   December 31, 1988
March 23, 1994   February 18, 1985   March 22, 1923
September 28, 1972

1. _____Team USA won Olympic gold at Lake Placid, NY.
2. _____Wayne Gretzky scored his 802nd goal to pass Gordie Howe.
3. _____Bobby Hull signed with the NHL-rival World Hockey Association.
4. _____The legendary Foster Hewitt broadcast the first hockey game.
5. _____Paul Henderson scored for Canada at the Summit Series.
6. _____Jacques Plante became the first goalie to regularly wear a mask.
7. _____Scotty Bowman passed Dick Irvin as NHL's winningest coach.
8. _____Darryl Sittler set an all-time record by scoring a 10-point game.
9. _____Maurice Richard recorded the NHL's first 50-in-50 season.
10._____Mario Lemieux scored five goals in every possible way.

2

Number Crunch

WAYNE GRETZKY'S CAREER was not only defined by the number of records he smashed, but by how convincingly they were smashed. Since his retirement in 1999, for example, only two of Gretzky's 61 records have been broken (both by Mark Messier): most overtime assists and most All-Star game assists. Perhaps even more startling is that, in retirement, the Great One remains a record magnet. His 59 records were even boosted by one when Mario Lemieux came back from retirement to play and lowered his 2.005 career points-per-game average to 1.883, handing Gretzky, with 1.921, the NHL record. In this chapter, we crunch the numbers.

Answers are on page 25

2.1 As of 2006–07, how many consecutive seasons has Yanic Perreault led the NHL in faceoff-winning percentage?

A. Three straight times

B. Five straight times

C. Seven straight times

D. Nine straight times

2.2 What was the last unused sweater number in NHL history? (A rookie took it in 2006–07.)

A. No. 64

B. No. 74

C. No. 84

D. No. 94

2.3 **How much did the world's oldest hockey stick sell for on eBay in December 2006?**

A. Cdn.$10,000

B. Cdn.$100,000

C. Cdn.$1 million

D. More than Cdn.$2 million

2.4 **What is the fastest recorded time for an overtime goal in regular-season action?**

A. Four seconds

B. Six seconds

C. Eight seconds

D. 10 seconds

2.5 **How many stitches were needed to close up Washington defenseman Jamie Heward's face after he was cut by one of Mike Modano's skates in November 2006?**

A. Less than 50 stitches

B. 60 stitches

C. 80 stitches

D. More than 100 stitches

2.6 **Prior to March 19, 2006, when Toronto beat Pittsburgh 1–0 on a penalty-shot goal, how many years had it been since an NHL game was won 1–0 on a penalty shot?**

A. One year

B. 20 years

C. 70 years

D. No 1–0 game has ever been won on a penalty shot

2.7 How many Chicago head coaches did Denis Savard serve under as assistant coach before the Blackhawks hired him as head coach in 2006–07?

A. Only one head coach, Trent Yawney
B. Three head coaches
C. Five head coaches
D. Seven head coaches

2.8 How many fewer NHL regular-season games did Mark Messier play than Gordie Howe in his career?

A. Only one game less than Howe
B. 11 games less than Howe
C. 51 games less than Howe
D. 101 games less than Howe

2.9 Among the hundreds of players to play just one NHL game, how many scored a goal in their lone appearance?

A. None
B. Only one player, Brad Fast
C. Three players
D. 10 players

2.10 What distinction did Olli Jokinen hold in 2007–08?

A. He was the only Finnish-born NHL team captain
B. He is the highest-drafted Finnish player in NHL history
C. He led all active players in games without a playoff appearance
D. All of the above

2.11 How long was Neil Smith general manager of the New York Islanders?

A. Four hours

B. Four days

C. Four weeks

D. 40 days

2.12 Why was Ottawa's Peter Schaefer fined U.S.$2,500 in December 2006?

A. He waved a towel at officials

B. He sat down during the national anthem

C. He hit a player with his helmet

D. He threw a water bottle at a fan

2.13 Which Hart Trophy winner holds the record for amassing the most penalty minutes during the season he was elected MVP?

A. Gordie Howe in 1952

B. Jean Béliveau in 1956

C. Mark Messier in 1990

D. Chris Pronger in 2000

2.14 What is the most goals scored in a single season by a major junior player who never made the NHL?

A. 70 goals

B. 80 goals

C. 90 goals

D. 100 goals

2.15 What is the most number of penalty shots awarded to an NHLer in a season?

A. Four penalty shots

B. Five penalty shots

C. Six penalty shots

D. Seven penalty shots

2.16 What is the most number of points scored by a player in a season-opening game?

A. Five points

B. Six points

C. Seven points

D. Eight points

2.17 How much money did Teemu Selanne offer former Winnipeg Jet teammate Randy Carlyle for his No. 8 jersey?

A. U.S.$100

B. U.S.$1,000

C. U.S.$10,000

D. U.S.$100,000

2.18 Which NHLer's salary accounted for more of his team's payroll than any other player's in 2006–07?

A. Tampa Bay forward Brad Richards's

B. New York Rangers forward Jaromir Jagr's

C. Detroit defenseman Nicklas Lidstrom's

D. Boston defenseman Zdeno Chara's

2.19 In April 2005, a group of Canadians took hockey to new heights by playing a game of shinny on what mountain?

A. Mount Aconcagua, Argentina

B. Mount McKinley, Alaska

C. Mount Everest, Nepal

D. Mount Vinson-Massif, Antarctica

Number Crunch

Answers

2.1 **C. Seven straight times**

There is little statistical evidence that faceoffs win hockey games, which may explain why the art of winning draws is one of hockey's least appreciated one-on-one skills—one that gets little attention in player stat boxes and game reports. Further, since nearly every NHL team is almost average in faceoff wins, other aspects of play (such as giveaways and takeaways) tend to be more important and make up the difference after losing a faceoff. Still, this showdown to gain puck possession is played out about 60 times every game and, on occasion, leads to a crucial goal or prevents another team from scoring. Yet only a handful of forwards are very good at it; anyone with 53 per cent or better is usually a top 20 player on the draw. So it is remarkable that Yanic Perreault has been leading the league with a figure higher than 61 per cent for seven seasons—almost as long as the statistic has been officially charted. How many players have accomplished anything close to that?

Yanic Perreault: Faceoff Gunslinger

SEASON	FO TOTAL	FO WINS	FO LOSSES	FO PERCENTAGE
1999–00	987	610	377	61.80
2000–01	1,055	661	394	62.65
2001–02	1,485	910	575	61.27
2002–03	1,156	727	429	62.88
2003–04	861	561	300	65.15
2005–06	899	559	340	62.18
2006–07	806	506	300	62.77

2.2   C. No. 84

Even though he ranked 11th in points among rookies,
Montreal's Guillaume Latendresse still drew considerable
attention in 2006–07. Hall of Fame goalie Patrick Roy got on
Latendresse's case, saying the teenager was only playing with
the Canadiens because he was French, to which Latendresse
fired back: "I thought I was the one who was 19 years old." To
prove his readiness, after replacing Chris Higgins on the Habs'
top line, the rookie then scored four goals in a five-game span.
But his first claim to fame came in his debut on October 6,
2006, when he wore No. 84 on the back of his Habs jersey—
the first player to wear the number. Eighty-four was the last
unused number in the NHL. At least one NHLer has donned
every other number from one to the now-retired 99.

2.3   D. More than Cdn.$2 million

The story is as fascinating as any heirloom yarn on TV's popular *Antiques Roadshow*. At the age of nine, Gordon Sharpe was
given an old, gnarled hockey stick by his great uncle. That
great uncle's grandfather—Alexander Rutherford Sr.—had

hand-carved the stick out of hickory wood from his family's Ontario farm, between 1852 and 1856. Sharpe played road hockey with the family relic, and, when he grew up, had it authenticated at the Hockey Hall of Fame—where, at the time, the oldest stick dated only to 1881. After an appraisal, Sharpe then put the twig on eBay, where it sold for Cdn.$2.2 million. The stick's new owner, a Canadian who remains anonymous, offered it to the Hall for display. The proceeds of the sale went to Sharpe's World Charity Award program to advance charity work in Canada and abroad.

2.4   B. Six seconds

When Philadelphia's Simon Gagne scored seven seconds into overtime against the New York Rangers on January 5, 2006, it was just one second off the mark held by Mats Sundin—who fired the fastest overtime goal in NHL history a mere six seconds into the extra period against St. Louis on December 30, 1995. Gagne's quick game-winner left Ranger goalie Kevin Weekes crushed. "I had too much time to think about it. I should have stuck to my guns, relied on my instincts and butterflied rather than go down on one knee. Obviously, it's deflating, not only for the guys, who played so well, but for the fans," said Weekes. The fastest goal from the start of a game is five seconds (shared by three players); the fastest goal from the start of a period is four seconds (held by two players).

2.5   D. More than 100 stitches

He joked afterwards about getting "an extreme makeover," but few NHL injuries have been more frightening than the facial laceration Jamie Heward suffered in a Washington–Dallas game on November 30, 2006. One of Mike Modano's skates carved open the left side of Heward's face—from the bridge of his nose to the outside of his left eye. The 35-year-old fell immediately, but got up and skated off just as quickly. "We knew it was serious," said Capitals coach Glen Hanlon. "Normally if you are hurt pretty bad, you just try to stay down. When you are hurt real seriously, there is a kind of mechanism that says, 'I've got to go and get some help.'" Heward's cut caused more damage than first feared. A 45-minute procedure turned into nearly five hours of surgery after doctors discovered Heward's nose cartilage had been severed along with a superficial nerve and artery. More than 100 stitches were needed to sew up the gash. Yet Heward was game-ready and wearing a visor against Atlanta by December 15, just five games after his horrific injury.

2.6   C. 70 years

Yes, there was a series of blackouts, an electrical fire that resulted in a 40-minute game delay, fans chanting "New A-Re-Naaaa" and a video review of a nullified goal—all of which had Toronto's Chad Kilger admitting "it was a bizarre game, for sure." But the Mellon Center game's highlight was still Kilger's penalty-shot goal, which came after the forward was tripped up by defenseman Rob Scuderi on a breakaway against Penguin goalie Marc-Andre Fleury. On the ensuing penalty shot, the Toronto forward backed Fleury deep into the net and wristed a shot past his blocker and inside the left post. The only score of the game, Kilger's goal also avenged the Maple Leafs' 1–0 loss to the Rangers on a penalty shot by Bert Connelly on January 16, 1936. It was the only other occasion a 1–0 game was won on a penalty shot.

2.7   D. Seven head coaches

If numbers were kept on this sort of thing, Denis Savard

probably set an NHL record when he became Chicago's head coach in November 2006. In Savard's nine years as an assistant, he saw Craig Hartsburg, Dirk Graham, Lorne Molleken, Bob Pulford, Alpo Suhonen, Brian Sutter and Trent Yawney go through Chicago's revolving door of head coaches. Savard had a hot start behind the bench and became only the second coach in club history to win his first three games. Still, he will forever battle the old theory that superstar athletes don't make good head coaches.

2.8   B. 11 games less than Howe

The NHL lockout of 2004–05 prematurely ended the careers of several veteran stars, including Ron Francis and Al MacInnis. Even that warrior of a quarter-century of hockey, Mark Messier, hung up his blades in 2005 after watching the league waste the year. In the end, Moose played 1,756 games, just 11 games shy of Gordie Howe's magic number of 1,767. Only 11 games. But that's probably okay with Messier, who could have broken Howe's famous record by playing in 2005–06. As Glen Sather remembered: "He was never the guy who wanted to get on the ice for an empty-net goal. He always let somebody else do that. He was a great team guy." And we would be remiss if we excluded the fact that 11 was the same number Messier wore on his back during his distinguished career, from 1979–80 to 2003–04.

2.9   C. Three players

Although not household names, Rolly Huard, Dean Morton and Brad Fast still lived the dream of playing in the world's best league, if only for one game. But Huard, Morton and Fast are more than one-game wonders, they are the NHL's only goal-a-game one-game wonders. Huard played with Toronto on December 14, 1930, and scored in a 7–3 loss to Boston; Morton notched a goal for Detroit in a 10–7 loss to Calgary on October 5, 1989; and Fast made his debut in Carolina's final game of 2003–04, scoring the game-tying goal with 2:26 left in regulation time in a 6–6 finish against Florida. And though the whys and what ifs surrounding their departures may haunt Huard and Morton for years, Fast could make it back to the NHL. In 2006–07, he was playing with the Swiss club Langnau.

2.10 C. He led all active players in games without a playoff appearance

Olli Jokinen's early career took him to three teams in three years, which should have improved the odds of seeing some postseason action from perennial contenders the Los Angeles Kings, New York Islanders and Florida Panthers. But the moves only meant earlier green times for the Panthers captain. As of 2006–07, after eight NHL seasons and change, Jokinen had appeared in 641 games—the highest total among all active NHLers and about one season shy of record holder Guy Charron's 734 matches without a playoff sniff. Ironically, Charron is an assistant coach with the Panthers. As for clues A and B, Jokinen was the third Finn to be named an NHL team captain (after Saku Koivu and Teppo Numminen); his third overall selection at the 1997 draft only ties him with Aki Berg (third overall in 1995) as the highest-drafted Finn.

2.11 D. 40 days

Neil Smith is no stranger to head cases. His finest hour was delivering a 1994 Stanley Cup to long-suffering Rangers fans while working with control-freak coach Mike Keenan. But no experience prepared him for Charles Wang, the self-proclaimed non-hockey guy and unconventional Islanders owner who hired Smith as general manager in the summer of 2006, then axed him 40 days later. The story goes that Smith clashed with Wang's committee approach, which had every front-office manager reporting directly to him. Still, in less than six weeks, Smith got a lot done, including the hiring of Chris Simon, Tom Poti, Mike Sillinger and Brendan Witt. Smith was replaced by backup goalie Garth Snow, who had zero expertise in the business side of the game.

2.12 A. He waved a towel at officials

Knowing a little hockey history can save a lot of dough. Peter Schaefer was just five years old when late coach Roger Neilson made hockey headlines by waving a towel in mock surrender at referees during the 1982 playoffs. Had Schaefer known of Neilson's faux pas, he might not have made the same mistake with his own stick-and-towel wave after a string of penalty calls in a Washington–Ottawa tilt on December 6, 2006. "I didn't think about it at all until I got off the ice and I had about five text messages from some buddies," said Schaefer. Within a day, the Ottawa forward also had a Post-it Note on his locker to call NHL executive Colin Campbell, who fined him $2,500—considerably less than the $11,000 Neilson and the Vancouver Canucks were penalized in 1982. During the 2006 game, referees Kevin Pollack and Justin St. Pierre assessed 11 penalties to each team. The Capitals won 6–2.

2.13 B. Jean Béliveau in 1956

You could win a few bucks in a bar bet with this one. All of the likely candidates—Gordie Howe, Eddie Shore, Mark Messier, Chris Pronger—rank far behind Jean Béliveau for box time during the years they won their Harts. The Montreal

Canadiens MVP led the league with 47 goals and 88 points in 1955–56, despite compiling 143 penalty minutes in 70 games, a heavy total for a guy associated with clean play. Béliveau's closest challenger is Bobby Clarke, who, though never associated with clean play, holds two spots among top penalty-earning MVPs. However, the all-time leader according to penalty minutes per game is Nels Stewart. In 1925–26, the Montreal Maroons rookie logged 119 PIM in just 36 games, an average of 3.31 per game.

Most PIM in a Season by NHL MVPS*

PLAYER	YEAR	TEAM	GP	PIM
Jean Béliveau	1956	Montreal	70	143
Bobby Clarke	1976	Philadelphia	76	136
Bobby Orr	1970	Boston	76	125
Bobby Clarke	1975	Philadelphia	80	125
Nels Stewart	1926	Montreal Maroons	36	119

*Including 2006–07

2.14   D. 100 goals

The name Gary MacGregor is not well known, but MacGregor's career on-ice and in the record books is connected with many of hockey's elite. That's because in his final junior year, 1973–74, MacGregor scored 100 goals in 66 games with Cornwall, a feat bested only by junior stars such as Mario Lemieux, Guy Lafleur and Pat LaFontaine. MacGregor was also one of Wayne Gretzky's first professional teammates, with the WHA Indianapolis Racers, before the team folded in 1978. So what led one of the CHL's highest-scoring players, a prospect who supposedly never lost a fight in junior hockey, to fall short of an NHL career? Apparently, in 1974, MacGregor was offered bigger money to play in the WHA, where he would get more ice time than with his NHL-drafted team, the Montreal Canadiens (where the competition for a roster spot at centre included Lafleur, Jacques Lemaire and Pete Mahovlich). So, rather than languish in the minors while waiting for an NHL break, MacGregor made the WHA his career choice and signed with the Chicago Cougars—and never played in the NHL. Still, he did net a 92–70–162 record in 251 WHA games between 1974 and 1979. Among junior players, the next-highest scorer without an NHL career is Jacques Locas Jr., who had 99 goals in 67 games with the Quebec Remparts in 1973-74.

2.15   B. Five penalty shots

The new rules to curb obstruction turned 2005–06 into a banner year for penalty shots. The NHL total of 103 shots almost doubled the previous record high of 57 in 2003–04 and far outdistanced 2006–07's 70 shots. The proliferation of one-on-one situations in 2005–06 also set records in individual efforts not seen since the penalty-shot rule was first enforced in 1934–35. Carolina's Eric Cole was awarded five penalty shots for the first time in league history, while Nashville's Steve Sullivan had four, equalling Ebbie Goodfellow's record count of four in 1934–35. Goodfellow scored only once, as did Sullivan; but Cole notched two, on November 9, 2005 and on January 21, 2006.

2.16   B. Six points

A whack of players in league history have scored five points in season openers, including Andy Bathgate, Phil Esposito and Gilbert Perreault. But the only player to notch six is Pittsburgh forward Kevin Stevens, who scored twice and had four assists in a 7–4 win against Washington on October 5, 1990. Linemate John Cullen recorded five assists in the game.

2.17   C. U.S.$10,000

How much is a number worth? In 2006–07, Selanne reflected on just that while playing alongside present-day Anaheim coach Randy Carlyle. Carlyle wore Winnipeg's No. 8, Selanne's jersey number with Jokerit in his native Finland. So Selanne took his Finnish soccer number, No. 13, but not before trying to coax the longtime Jet out of his famous digit. "In Winnipeg, I once offered him [Carlyle] $10,000 to wear his No. 8 jersey, and he refused," said Selanne. But Carlyle retired in 1993, and a year later Selanne got No. 8—free of charge.

2.18   A. Tampa Bay forward Brad Richards's

Playing in a capped league with a U.S.$44-million ceiling on salaries didn't leave the Lightning with a lot of wiggle room after they won the Stanley Cup in 2004. The price of success in the new NHL was a $20-million hit for three forwards: Brad Richards ($7.8 million), Vincent Lacavalier ($6.9 million) and Martin St. Louis ($5.2 million), or almost 50 per cent of Tampa's payroll. Meanwhile, the rest of the team's 2006–07 bench was filled with a supporting cast of mostly minimum-wage earners who scrimped by on $650,000 or less. Richards, the highest-paid player, gobbled up the greatest percentage of his team's salary; Nicklas Lidstrom made $7.6 million; Zdeno Chara, $7.5 million. As for Jaromir Jagr, who took home $8.36 million, just $4.94 million went against the Rangers' cap. The remaining $3.4 million was Washington's headache as part of its 2004 trade with New York. (Fortunately, the Capitals' portion of Jagr's salary is excluded when calculating the team's cap space.)

2.19   C. Mount Everest, Nepal

On the morning of April 11, 2004, a group of Canadian climbers staged a game of shinny atop Mount Everest's Khumbu Glacier. Played in calm weather in front of a crowd of spectators at an elevation of 17,575 feet, it set a record for the highest game of hockey ever played—a tribute to the original 1972 Summit Series between Canada and the USSR. (In fact, prior to leaving for Everest, the Canadians were presented with original Team Canada jerseys by Ron Ellis, a member of Canada's 1972 Summit Series team and a former Toronto Maple Leaf star.) And though the Canadians were slated to play a team of Russian climbers, when the Russians didn't show, the Canadian climbers took on a squad composed of players from Australia, Nepal and the USA. Besides the rarefied elevation, the game also featured some other oddities: the referee was a sherpa named Tsherling, a crevasse doubled as the penalty box and, at one point, the action was interrupted by three yaks that decided to cross the rink—or "glink," as the Canadians dubbed it. Canada won the record-breaking match, 21–13.

Lowering the Boom

THE LONGEST SUSPENSION in NHL history was
handed down to Chris Simon, after the Islanders
enforcer deliberately swung his stick and delivered a two-handed
blow with "intent to injure" during a game in March 2007. Simon
received a minimum suspension of 25 games, including 15 games
during 2006–07 and the entire playoffs. In this game, match the
banished players and their time served on the left with their targets
on the right. The dates of the incidents may help your rulings.

Solutions are on page 120

PART 1

1. Chris Simon (25 games)
2. Marty McSorley (23 games)
3. Gordie Dwyer (23 games)
4. Dale Hunter (21 games)
5. Todd Bertuzzi (20 games)
6. Tom Lysiak (20 games)

A. Donald Brashear (February 2000)
B. Tripping an official (October 1983)
C. Pierre Turgeon (May 1993)
D. Steve Moore (March 2004)
E. Ryan Hollweg (March 2007)
F. Abusing officials and exiting the
   penalty box to fight (September 2000)

PART 2

1. Brad May (20 games)
2. Eddie Shore (16 games)
3. Maurice Richard (15 games)
4. Wilf Paiement (15 games)
5. Dave Brown (15 games)
6. Tony Granato (15 games)

A. Striking an official (March 1955)
B. Dennis Polonich (October 1978)
C. Tomas Sandstrom (November 1987)
D. Steve Heinze (November 2000)
E. Neil Wilkinson (February 1994)
F. Ace Bailey (December 1933)

3

The Deep End

THEY'RE A DYING BREED: the nutty and neurotic netminder. True, today's elite goalies still follow pregame rituals and even refuse to meet media on game day, but the strangeness factor has disappeared. No one pukes before games as Glenn Hall did; or showers between periods, a Gary Smith custom; or even believes in reincarnation like Gilles Gratton, who was convinced he was a soldier during the Spanish Inquisition. And Patrick Roy, the quirkiest of all the bobbing and twitching head cases? He hasn't spoken to his goal posts in years. With the exceptions of nutbar Ed Belfour and the cockroach-eating Ray Emery, the wackiness is over, gone with the centre redline and $12 tickets. It's kind of a shame, but the crazies have been replaced with more balanced goalies who benefit from all that specialized coaching. The deep end has never been so shallow.

Answers are on page 41

3.1 Who wore two different masks and sets of equipment in 2006–07: one to go with his team's regular uniforms and one to match his team's vintage third jerseys?

A. Ryan Miller of the Buffalo Sabres

B. Dwayne Roloson of the Edmonton Oilers

C. Roberto Luongo of the Vancouver Canucks

D. Marc-Andre Fleury of the Pittsburgh Penguins

3.2 What sports figure's image was Ottawa goalie Ray Emery asked to remove from his mask in February 2006?

A. Tennis babe Maria Sharapova

B. Baseball slugger Barry Bonds

C. Basketball bad boy Dennis Rodman

D. Boxer and ear-biter Mike Tyson

3.3 Who had his prestigious record for most wins in a season broken by Martin Brodeur in 2006–07?

A. Terry Sawchuk of the Detroit Red Wings

B. Bernie Parent of the Philadelphia Flyers

C. Ken Dryden of the Montreal Canadiens

D. Patrick Roy of the Colorado Avalanche

3.4 Who tried to become the first goalie in NHL history to take a faceoff in 2006–07?

A. Rick DiPietro of the New York Islanders

B. Marty Turco of the Dallas Stars

C. Ray Emery of the Ottawa Senators

D. Manny Legace of the St. Louis Blues

3.5 What goaltending rarity is shared by Alex Auld and Miikka Kiprusoff?

A. They each recorded a shutout without a win

B. They each registered an assist in the same game

C. They each played in home jerseys during the same game

D. They each received game misconducts for fighting

3.6 What is the single-season record for victories by a goalie aged 40 or older?

A. Less than 15 wins

B. Between 15 and 25 wins

C. Between 25 and 35 wins

D. More than 35 wins

3.7 **Who was the first goalie to coach an NHL team?**

A. Hugh Lehman of the Chicago Blackhawks

B. Emile Francis of the New York Rangers

C. Percy LeSueur of the Hamilton Tigers

D. Gerry Cheevers of the Boston Bruins

3.8 **Which goalie said, "Excuse my French. A bigger net is crap. It's ridiculous, even stupid"—when asked his opinion about enlarging the goal net in 2006–07?**

A. Jose Theodore of the Colorado Avalanche

B. Cristobal Huet of the Montreal Canadiens

C. Martin Brodeur of the New Jersey Devils

D. Marc-Andre Fleury of the Pittsburgh Penguins

3.9 **Who is considered to be hockey's first goalie "closer"— since he came into the game just for the shootout?**

A. Jean-Sebastian Giguere of the Anaheim Ducks

B. Kari Lehtonen of the Atlanta Thrashers

C. Mike Morrison of the Edmonton Oilers

D. Eugeni Nabokov of the San Jose Sharks

3.10 **What is the longest stretch of consecutive shutouts at home recorded by a goalie?**

A. Three home shutouts

B. Four home shutouts

C. Five home shutouts

D. Six home shutouts

3.11 Who broke Martin Brodeur's record of most minutes played in a season in 2006–07?

A. Andrew Raycroft of the Toronto Maple Leafs

B. Miikka Kiprusoff of the Calgary Flames

C. Roberto Luongo of the Vancouver Canucks

D. Martin Brodeur of the New Jersey Devils

3.12 What was Philadelphia goalie Robert Esche referring to when he said, in October 2006, "It's an empty place"?

A. The office of ex-Flyers general manager Bobby Clarke

B. Philadelphia's home rink, Wachovia Center

C. The head of ex-Flyers coach Ken Hitchcock

D. Derian Hatcher's jock support

3.13 Who earned the moniker "the King"?

A. Ryan Miller of the Buffalo Sabres

B. Henrik Lundqvist of the New York Rangers

C. Mathieu Garon of the Los Angeles Kings

D. Dominik Hasek of the Detroit Red Wings

3.14 In 2006–07, which goalie with connections to the old Winnipeg Jets wore a mask featuring players from that team?

A. Curtis Joseph of the Phoenix Coyotes

B. Nikolai Khabibulin of the Chicago Blackhawks

C. Robert Esche of the Philadelphia Flyers

D. Mikael Tellqvist of the Phoenix Coyotes

3.15 Which NHL all-time record did Martin Brodeur break in 2006–07?

A. Most career wins

B. Most career shutouts

C. Most career overtime wins

D. All of the above

3.16 **Among the 26,694 shots on Hall of Fame goalie Gump Worsley during his 21-year NHL career, how many did he face while wearing a mask?**

A. Less than 200 shots

B. About 2,000 shots

C. About 10,000 shots

D. None of them; Worsley never wore a mask

3.17 **In what year does Rick DiPietro's landmark 2006 contract with the New York Islanders expire?**

A. In 2008–09

B. In 2012–13

C. In 2016–17

D. In 2020–21

The Deep End

Answers

3.1 **C. Roberto Luongo of the Vancouver Canucks**

Roberto Luongo made a major fashion statement in 2006–07 as the first NHL goalie to don two different sets of equipment, depending on which jersey his team was wearing that game. When the Canucks were clad in their regular killer-whale jerseys, Luongo suited up with a mask featuring the Vancouver skyline, a bear tearing through a goalie mask and the Lions

Gate Bridge. And on those nights when the club donned its throwback blue, green and white jerseys, Luongo wore a set of colour-coordinated pads and a cream-coloured vintage mask that was designed to resemble those of the early 1970s, when the Canucks entered the league. The otherwise unadorned mask sported a graphic of that bearded lumberjack-on-skates figure Johnny Canuck, the cartoon character the team was named after, on its side.

3.2 D. Boxer and ear-biter Mike Tyson

Ray Emery's mask of Mike Tyson lasted all of one game, a 5–0 loss to Boston on January 30, 2006. If the Bruins' pounding wasn't enough to prompt Emery to reconsider his design choice, Senators GM John Muckler provided the knockout blow when he reminded Emery, an avid boxing fan, that Tyson was a convicted rapist and abuser of women. "Growing up, he always had boxers on his helmet, and I appreciate that Tyson was an idol to him as a boxer," said Muckler. "But after discussions about Tyson's past…[Emery] said he'll no longer wear it [the boxer] on his face mask." The Tyson illustration was quickly painted over with a safer pick: an image of Canadian boxing legend George Chuvalo.

3.3 B. Bernie Parent of the Philadelphia Flyers

When the NHL decided to abolish ties with shootout victories (and overtime, to a lesser degree), a slew of team and individual records were bound to fall, including one of hockey's most famous: Bernie Parent's celebrated 47 wins in 1973–74. But even before Martin Brodeur topped Parent's mark with his 48th victory in 2006–07 (beating Parent's beloved Flyers, no less), the ugly "a"-word was being mentioned. Would an asterisk in the record books really clear the air over who had more wins in a season? Parent himself wouldn't hear of it: "You still have the five minutes of overtime and then the shootout, so you still have to win." Still, his 33-year record was hammered not once, but twice in 2006–07. Vancouver's Roberto Luongo equalled Parent with his own 47-win season, notching 11 overtime and five shootout victories, and 13 of Brodeur's 48 wins came either in overtime (3) or the shootout (10). Meanwhile, Parent was limited by 12 ties and a 78-game season in 1973–74. "I wish that anyone that ever looks at the record would mention Bernie Parent and his effort with a shorter season and no shootouts, still having 47 wins," said Brodeur.

3.4 B. Marty Turco of the Dallas Stars

Marty Turco's stickhandling abilities have earned him 10 assists in his NHL career, but his offensive talents with the paddle almost won him an unusual NHL first in a Dallas–Los Angeles game on October 14, 2006. It happened during the third period, with both teams playing four-on-four, and the faceoff opposite Turco. Dallas' Jeff Halpern got thrown out of the circle, and when no player skated into the dot to replace him, Turco seized the moment: with the linesman about to drop the puck, the netminder lined up opposite Los Angeles winger Derek Armstrong for the draw. The official motioned Turco out (under rule 76.1, a goalie cannot take faceoffs), thwarting history's first faceoff by a netminder. But the tactic bought time for Dallas, and Eric Lindros took the puck drop.

3.5 A. They each recorded a shutout without a win

There was a time in hockey when a shutout meant a win, or at least a tie, and Alex Auld and Miikka Kiprusoff know that better than any other goalies. On November 28, 2006, Auld stopped all Montreal Canadiens shooters during three periods and overtime, but surrendered two goals to Cristobal Huet's one in the shootout. "It's kind of crazy," said Auld, after his Panthers fell 1–0. "I never thought I'd get a shutout without a win." Kiprusoff was also left scratching his head after his shutout in Calgary's 1–0 loss to Philadelphia on December 6, 2005. It was the first scoreless tie decided by a shootout since the format was adopted.

3.6 D. More than 35 wins

Who in their right mind would sign a starting goalie who was 41 years old—even if his name was Dominik Hasek? The move by Detroit GM Ken Holland seemed uninspired, an act of desperation after giving up on Manny Legace and losing confidence in Chris Osgood. What's more, Hasek had already retired once, come back to Hockeytown and suffered an early season groin injury in 2003–04, sat out the lock-out year and then played flat with a 28–10–4 record in Ottawa in 2005–06. Yet the Czech wonder would prove every bit the warrior who backstopped Detroit with 41 wins in 2001–02—only a little older. Indeed, in 2006–07, Hasek set a new single-season record for wins by a plus-40-year-old goalie when he broke his previous league mark of 28 victories with his 29th in a 4–3 victory against the New York Rangers on February 5, 2007. Hasek would finish the year with a remarkable 38 victories. By then, he was 42 years old.

3.7 C. Percy LeSueur of the Hamilton Tigers

Despite their storied history as the game's most important and brightest players, few goaltenders have made the leap to bench boss. The first was Percy LeSueur, who never played in the NHL but won three Stanley Cups with the Ottawa

Senators before the league was formed in 1917. LeSueur's early fame came backstopping the Senators, but he later earned hockey titles as coach, manager, referee, inventor, arena manager and columnist. He was also the first manager of the old Detroit Olympia, the inventor of a gauntlet-type glove to protect a goalie's forearm and the inventor of the first goal net that could trap rising shots. As a reporter for the *Hamilton Spectator*, LeSueur also introduced the statistic "shots on goal" to his box scores. Yet despite his well-documented career of hockey firsts, LeSueur has never been credited as the first goalie to coach an NHL team, according to our research. In fact, it proved to be the low point in his Hall of Fame career, after he guided the outmatched Hamilton Tigers to last place with a 3–7–0 record in 10 games during 1923–24. Instead, the first NHL goalie to coach in the league was Hugh Lehman, who served Chicago for 21 games in 1927–28.

3.8 **A. Jose Theodore of the Colorado Avalanche**

Supersizing nets isn't a popular subject with goalies. Jose Theodore has made that clear, calling the idea "junk" and "bull___" in December 2006 after some enthusiasts suggested that larger nets would increase goal production. And Theodore isn't alone in his assessment. He has received unanimous support from his goaltending brethren, while hockey purists have taken the NHL to task, pointing out that goalies may be better trained and more bulked up with equipment, but they have already had their leg pads reduced in size and their stickhandling skills restricted to designated areas behind the net. All this, while shooters have become faster and better armed with composite metal sticks. The six-foot-by-four-foot goalie net has been a fixture in the NHL since 1917.

3.9   C. Mike Morrison of the Edmonton Oilers

Edmonton coach Craig MacTavish turned Mike Morrison into hockey's first bullpen closer, when he brought his rookie netminder into the game cold to replace started Ty Conklin for the shootout against Dallas on March 7, 2006. Conklin kicked out 23 of 26 shots through regulation and overtime for the Oilers, but MacTavish figured Morrison's 5–0 shootout record gave him the edge over Conklin in the game-deciding session. However, the Stars jumped all over Morrison, scoring two goals on two shots, while the Oilers were blanked on both their attempts against Marty Turco in the 4–3 loss. On October 26, 2006, Atlanta coach Bob Hartley also tried the switch, relieving Johan Hedberg for Karl Lehtonen. "Just like a baseball manager you have Mariano Rivera sitting on the bench, he's your closer, and Karl's our number one," said Hartley. In an earlier instance, Buffalo's Martin Biron replaced Mike Noronen *during* the shootout on November 22, 2005. But coach Lindy Ruff only made the move because Noronen hurt his groin in the third period and was favouring it in the shootout. It was the first goalie swap during a shootout. Interestingly, in all three games, the goalie coming in cold for the shootout allowed a goal in each of the first two shots he faced, and the opposition won the game.

3.10   B. Four home shutouts

After a string of three straight shutouts at Nassau Coliseum in December 2006, the Islanders' Rick DiPietro was poised to become only the second netminder in modern-era NHL hockey to record a fourth consecutive zero on home ice. All that stood in DiPietro's way were the New Jersey Devils and Martin Brodeur, the goalie who had just passed Glenn Hall's record of 84 shutouts with his 85th, for third best all-time. DiPietro played terrific, but Brodeur blanked the Isles with his 86th zero, a 2–0 win that halted DiPietro's home shutout streak at 191:04 in the December 30 game. After the final horn, the two goalies waved and DiPietro passed the puck down to Brodeur, who had just broken the 50,000-minute mark of his playing career. "That was a great gesture," said Brodeur. Six-team era goalie Terry Sawchuk is the only back-stopper to notch four straight shutouts at home. He did it in January 1955.

3.11   D. Martin Brodeur of the New Jersey Devils

Besides being an all-round nice guy and consummate team player, Martin Brodeur still relishes the spotlight of chasing individual NHL records—even if it's one of his own. Brodeur's NHL-record 4,697 minutes in 2006–07 topped his previous league mark of 4,555 in 2003–04. But the machine with the goalie pads has been known to take a night off, even if it means passing up another record. In New Jersey's last game of 2006–07 (a meaningless match for the playoff-bound Devils), Scott Clemmensen started, preventing Brodeur from tying Grant Fuhr's all-time mark of 79 games in one season. Brodeur fell short with 78 games.

3.12   C. The head of ex-Flyers coach Ken Hitchcock

Philadelphia's season-long ride into hell in 2006–07 can be traced to a pathetic off-ice power struggle between general manager Bob Clarke and head coach Ken Hitchcock over start-ing goalies. Instead of going with Clarke's choice of Esche, who played poorly in a season opener 4–0 loss, Hitchcock made Antero Niittymaki his starting netminder, a decision that triggered Esche to tell reporters: "I don't try getting into his (Hitchcock's) head. It's an empty place." Then, on October 17, Esche was hung out to dry by Hitchcock for all nine goals in a 9–1 thumping by the Sabres, suggesting that Hitchcock was sending a message to both Clarke and Esche. In the aftermath of that humiliating loss, Hitchcock was fired and Clarke resigned, only to return later in an administrative role. Yet neither Niittymaki or Esche proved to be the answer in 2006–07. Philadelphia finished in the basement with 56 points and its worst record in team history: 22–48–12.

3.13 B. Henrik Lundqvist of the New York Rangers

The New York media and Rangers fans nicknamed Lundqvist "the King," or King Henrik of Sweden, during 2005–06—when the Swedish backstopper set a new team rookie mark with 30 wins and led the league's freshmen in goals-against (2.24) and save percentage (.922). Lundqvist was also royal in the shootout, allowing nine goals on 37 shots for a league-best .757 among the top 10. He was twice named the NHL's defensive player of the week (October 23, January 16), played a major role in getting New York back in the playoffs and, during the 2006 Turin Olympics, found time to add another jewel to his crown: a gold medal for Sweden.

3.14 D. Mikael Tellqvist of the Phoenix Coyotes

Paying tribute to former players on goalie masks is a relatively new phenomenon. Among the first designs was Jocelyn Thibault's artful Jacques Plante mask from Thibeault's 1995–96 season with Montreal. Styled by artist Michel Lefebvre, the head gear depicted the "pretzel" style Fiberglas model worn by the legendary Plante, hockey's first masked goalie. Mikael

Tellqvist pursued a similar theme with illustrations of past greats on both his Toronto and Phoenix masks. Tellqvist's Maple Leafs face protector was distinguished by Johnny Bower and fellow Swede Borje Salming, while his Phoenix mask recognized the Coyotes' roots in Winnipeg with Jets legends Tomas Steen on the left side and Bobby Hull on the right. The next trend in mask art may favour more recently retired players. In February 2007, Montreal rookie Jaroslav Halak's mask featured Patrick Roy raising the Stanley Cup... in a Canadiens jersey.

3.15 C. Most career overtime wins

Barring unforeseen circumstances, Martin Brodeur is a lock to become both hockey's winningest goalie and its all-time leader in career shutouts. He just didn't do it in 2006–07, as we asked in our question. But just short of establishing new league marks in two of hockey's most prestigious records for netminders, Brodeur still had a banner year, charging past the likes of Jacques Plante and Glenn Hall to move within striking distance of Terry Sawchuk's once-thought-unassailable all-time mark of 103 shutouts, and beyond Ed Belfour and Sawchuk to put Roy's 551-win record squarely in his crosshairs. How fast is Brodeur doing all this? When Brodeur tied Sawchuk's 447 wins on October 6, he was, at 34 years, 153 days of age, the youngest to reach that mark— and he did it in the fewest number of games, 814. "That's the one you want," the long-time Devils goalie said. "Hockey is a team game and it's all about winning." Lost in the scramble was Brodeur's 45th career overtime win, which tops Roy's all-time mark of 44. It happened in a 6–5 OT victory against Philadelphia on February 1, 2007.

3.16 A. Less than 200 shots

He was the pot-bellied goalie who drank "only rye," smoked
like a chimney between periods and possessed the sharpest
sense of humour in the game. But on-ice his athleticism
belied everything that he said or did elsewhere. We know
all this because Gump Worsley openly shared his warts, for
which he was loved by fans. But the Gumper wasn't truly
appreciated until he was traded to Montreal after a punish-
ing decade in the shooting galley of the cellar-dwelling New
York Rangers. Once, when asked which team gave him the
most trouble, he shot back: "the Rangers." And he was right.
Worsley averaged 35.0 shots per game, compared to Glenn
Hall (29.7) and Jacques Plante (28.2) between 1954–55 and
1962–63. But his trade to the Canadiens changed everything.
It not only earned him respectability as a clutch performer,
but four Stanley Cups, a Vezina Trophy with Charlie Hodge
and his lone First All-Star nomination. Still, Worsley's game
was anything but elegant. He flung his small roly-poly frame
about with great timing, and often stacked his pads—a
Worsley innovation—to stop a shot. The goalie who famously
said, "My face is my mask," also stared down 26,694 shots, less
than 200 of them while begrudgingly wearing face protection
in the final six NHL games of his illustrious career. Worsley
could also have been the last NHL netminder to go barefaced
(that title would go to Andy Brown), but he decided to slip one
on after Minnesota's Cesare Maniago convinced him it might
be a good idea to protect his eyes, as retirement was just
months away. Worsley claims he wore his first mask on March
17, 1974, in a 5–2 loss, while facing 36 shots against Buffalo. It
was his 855th NHL game, an amazing 14 seasons after Jacques
Plante ushered in the era of the masked goalie in 1959.

D. In 2020–21

If lotteries are just self-imposed taxes for stupid people,
what would be the equivalent idiocy for billionaire sports
owners and their millionaire athletes? When Rick DiPietro
signed his staggering U.S.$67.5-million, 15-year contract
in September 2006, for example, it drew a lot of attention
around the league, and a lot of laughs. DiPietro may be worth
his guaranteed annual salary of U.S.$4.5 million, but will he
be worth it every season until the deal is complete in 2020–21?
The argument goes: If DiPietro is that good and has a Patrick
Roy-like career, then the Islanders protect themselves from a
potential U.S.$7-million salary, an annual figure that the New
York goalie could demand after an exceptional year under
shorter-term contracts. For DiPietro, the upside is guaranteed
money and payment in full should he retire because of injury.
On the other end, there's the added pressure of a huge contract. And what's to motivate him, as one general manager
wondered: "He's never going to have another negotiation in
his career." Both sides are also gambling on what happens
in the marketplace. If revenues drastically improve, DiPietro
has undervalued himself. A drop in the marketplace means
owner Charles Wang is getting fleeced. The colossal deal is
the longest in NHL history (except for Wayne Gretzky's 21-year
deal, which included personal services stipulations), and tops
the 10-year, U.S.$87.5-million contract inked between Wang's
Islanders and Alexei Yashin in 2001.

Not-Ready-for-Prime-Time Records

OFTEN THE MOST REMARKABLE NHL records aren't achieved by hockey's elite players. Wayne Gretzky didn't notch the largest goal increase between two seasons in league history, for example; and Martin Brodeur hasn't even come close to topping the record for most consecutive games allowing two goals or less. The flip side is that some superstars are less-known for their exceptional, yet unofficial, records, such as Brett Hull's stats total in 1990–91. Match the NHLers and their unheralded records below.

Solutions are on page 120

PART 1 (SKATERS)

Brett Hull   Owen Nolan   Pavel Bure
Tom Bladon   Doug Smail   Tiger Williams

1. Most goals without a power-play goal in one season: 31 goals
2. Highest percentage of team's total goals in one season: 29.5 per cent
3. Most goals by a penalty-minute leader in one season: 35 goals
4. Largest goal hike between two seasons (minimum 50 games): 39 goals
5. Highest plus-minus by a player in one game: plus-10
6. Largest goals-to-assists differential in one season: 41 goals

PART 2 (GOALIES)

Jacques Plante   Frank Brophy   Bill Durnan
Michel Belhumeur   Terry Sawchuk   Ken McAuley

1. Most consecutive games allowing two goals or less: 18 games
2. Most wins by a rookie goalie in one season: 44 victories
3. Most goals allowed by a goalie in one season: 310 goals
4. Most games without a win in one season: 35 games
5. Fewest defeats in one season (playing minimum 50 games): 5 losses
6. Most goals allowed by a goalie in one game: 16 goals

4

True or False?

A **MONG EUROPEAN-TRAINED PLAYERS,** Teppo Numminen leads all NHLers in games played, including Jari Kurri. True or False? *True.* For a guy who admitted "I really didn't plan to stay here that long," Numminen has had quite a career. The Finnish rearguard figured on playing only a year or two in the NHL, but stayed for 18-plus seasons. In fact, he set the league record for most games played by a European on November 13, 2006, when he surpassed country-man Jari Kurri's mark by skating in his 1,252nd match. In the game, Numminen also registered his 600th career point in Buffalo's 7–4 win against Carolina.

Answers are on page 57

4.1 **Eighteen-year-old rookie Jordan Staal scored more goals than his older brother Eric Stall did in 2006–07.** True or False?

4.2 **No Selke Trophy winner as best defensive forward has ever scored 1,000 points.** True or False?

4.3 **As of 2006–07, the last scoring champion from an Original Six team is Guy Lafleur, in 1977–78.** True or False?

4.4 **According to a study released in 2006, fighting in the NHL actually helps a team *win* games.** True or False?

53

4.5 In 2006–07, the Buffalo Sabres became the first team in NHL history to put player numbers on the front of its uniforms? True or False?

4.6 Although the Calgary Flames own the NHL record for most consecutive games without being shut out, the Los Angeles Kings hold the same mark—including playoff games. Each team's league record is 264 games. True or False?

4.7 Every time Wayne Gretzky played an NHL game on his birthday, he notched a point. True or False?

4.8 Chris Chelios became the first player in NHL history to still be playing in the league when he became eligible to collect his NHL pension in 2006–07. True or False?

4.9 Before Pittsburgh's Sidney Crosby, Jordan Staal and Kristopher Letang scored in a 2006–07 game, no team had ever iced three teenage goal scorers in the same match. True or False?

4.10 In 2006, eBay auctioned off a figurine of Buffalo goalie Clint Malarchuk that depicts the night in March 1989 when his throat was slit by a skate and he almost died on the ice. True or False?

4.11 When the net is intentionally or accidentally dislodged from its moorings, the referee whistles the play dead. True or False?

4.12 The gold-medal men's hockey game between Canada and the U.S. at the 2002 Winter Olympics drew the largest television audience in Canadian history. True or False?

4.13 The first NHL team to release a licensed version of the Monopoly board game was the New York Rangers. True or False?

4.14 In 2006–07, Ottawa's Daniel Alfredsson became the first NHL player in 86 years to score game-winning goals in four straight games. True or False?

4.15 No player has ever led the NHL in plus-minus in one season and then finished last in the league in the category in another year. True or False?

4.16 As of 2006–07, the Montreal Canadiens have not issued another player Patrick Roy's No. 33 since Roy was traded in December 1995. True or False?

4.17 Ted Nolan's first return to Buffalo as coach of the Islanders resulted in a New York win. True or False?

4.18 The Philadelphia Flyers' famous 35-game unbeaten streak is the longest among the four major league sports. True or False?

4.19 When Henrik and Joel Lundqvist played against each other in a December 2006 match between the New York Rangers and Dallas Stars, it marked the first time a goaltender faced his twin brother in NHL history. True or False?

4.20 Pittsburgh goalie Marc-Andre Fleury set a record in 2006–07, by becoming the first NHL netminder to win eight games against one opponent in a season without suffering a loss or tie. True or False?

4.21 No player has ever won the Calder Trophy as the NHL's outstanding rookie and then spent the next season in the minors. True or False?

4.22 Curtis Joseph has appeared in more playoff games than any goalie in NHL history who has not won a Stanley Cup. True or False?

4.23 In what was considered a sportscasting first, both the play-by-play announcer and colour commentator called an NHL game from ice level between the benches. It happened in 2006–07. True or False?

4.24 A medical report on bodychecking in hockey leagues for 11-year-old boys found *no* evidence that bodychecking increases the rate of serious injuries. True or False?

4.25 The old Colorado Rockies was the first sports team to play the rock anthem "Rock and Roll" (Part 2)—also known as "The Hey Song"—during home games. True or False?

4.26 Despite the NHL's efforts to increase scoring, goal totals declined between 2005–06 and 2006–07. True or False?

4.27 Sidney Crosby is the youngest player in history voted to an NHL All-Star game since fan balloting began in 1986. True or False?

Answers

4.1   False

Anyone who thought Jordan Staal would challenge his
brother in goal totals in 2006–07, raise your hands. No one?
Jordan's first season with Pittsburgh surprised most fans,
including the Penguins, who got 29 goals from the 18-year-
old—just one less than the 30 that Carolina earned with
his brother, Eric. The numbers had people talking family
dynasty—and sibling rivalry. Was Eric just suffering from a
Stanley Cup hangover, or did Jordan instantly mature into a
bonafide NHLer? "I told him, I'm coming for him," said Jordan.
"But I didn't expect it to be this close."

4.2   False

When Rod Brind'Amour assisted on an Eric Cole goal against
Ottawa on November 4, 2006, the Carolina captain became
the 71st NHLer to amass 1,000 points and only the sixth Selke
winner to reach the millennium point mark. Brind'Amour
also claimed the best defensive forward award in 2006. The
other 1,000-point Selke winners are Bobby Clarke, Doug
Gilmour, Ron Francis, Steve Yzerman and two-time winner
Sergei Fedorov.

4.3   True

Say it ain't so. Outnumbered five to one in the 30-team NHL,
as of 2006–07, no club from the six-team era has had an NHL
scoring champion since Guy Lafleur scored 132 points for
Montreal in 1977–78.

4.4 **True**

The NHL fight club received some unexpected support from
an unlikely source in 2006, when a bunch of university profes-
sors dropped the gloves and cold-cocked the scrap-shy NHL
with a study that showed fighting is actually a good strategy
for team success. Admittedly, the report never concluded
"fighting is a good thing," but its statistical analysis did show
that major penalties—most often called for fights—increased
the total points held by a penalized player's team and lowered
the number of goals scored by their opposition. (Only major
penalties helped win games; minor penalties decreased a
team's success.) "It's clearly a rallying effect, and that's what
gets momentum to change in a game," said study author
Aju Fenn. The research, conducted by the Department of
Economics and Business at Colorado College in Colorado
Springs and the School of Business at the University of Sioux
Falls, crunched data for all NHL teams during five seasons,
1999–2000 through 2003–04. But critics of the report said
that the post-lockout NHL changed dramatically, with fights
between 2003–04 and 2005–06 dropping from 41 to 29 per
cent. Meanwhile, tough guy Georges Laraque, lamenting the
fact that only 11 teams regularly dressed enforcers in 2006–07,
called the NHL "a ballet league. They want to make this into a
European league," he fumed.

4.5 **False**

The Buffalo Sabres introduced a new jersey logo (dubbed the
"Buffaslug") in 2006–07 and added player numbers to the
front of their uniforms—a wrinkle copied later in the season by the Dallas Stars. But the Sabres are not the first NHL
team to do this. In 1936–37, the Boston Bruins put uniforms
numbers on both the backs and fronts of their jerseys, an

uninspiring concept the club stuck with for 12 years before introducing its familiar spoked-B crest.

4.6   True

Do players get a little more psyched when a team record is on the line? Sure. Just three games away from matching Calgary's non-shutout record of 264 games, Los Angeles, with 261 matches and counting, fell 5–0 to the club with the most to lose: Calgary, which cemented its NHL mark by zeroing the Kings on October 25, 1989. Interestingly, Los Angeles played another 57 games before another shutout loss, again to the Flames, and again 5–0. But the Kings salvaged a different league standard during that span when they recorded a 264-game non-shutout streak, including playoffs, March 15, 1986, to April 6, 1989.

4.7   True

Wayne Gretzky played on his birthday, January 26, 10 times between 1980 and 1999—and earned at least a point each game. The Great One celebrated with points in 1980 and 1983 vs. Toronto; 1982 and 1995 vs. St. Louis; 1985 vs. Pittsburgh; 1989 and 1991 vs. Vancouver; 1993 vs. San Jose; and 1998 and 1999 vs. Washington.

4.8   False

Chris Chelios is the second player to double dip at age 45, collecting an NHL pension while still receiving his U.S.$1.15-million salary from Detroit. In the process, Chelios joined Toronto backup netminder Johnny Bower, who, at age 45, started drawing pension cheques during his last season, 1969–70. The legendary Gordie Howe was also eligible for his NHL retirement fund at age 45, but Howe was playing alongside his sons in the WHA at the time. But when he returned to the NHL at age 51 in 1979–80, he too drew a league pension and salary. Chelios's first game as an NHL pensioner came in a 2–1 loss to St. Louis the day after his birthday, on January 26, 2007. He recorded 20 shifts in 17:11 of ice time, had one shot on net and blocked two more—not the accomplishments of a typical pensioner. Chelios was in his 23rd season.

4.9   False

Pittsburgh made the most of its lengthy stay in the NHL basement between 2001–02 and 2005–06, selecting the future of the franchise with five successive top-five draft picks: Ryan Whitney, fifth overall in 2002; Marc-Andre Fleury, first in 2003; Evgeni Malkin, second in 2004; Sidney Crosby, first in 2005, and Jordan Staal, second in 2006. The hockey world was soon hailing the Penguins' youth corps as the second coming of the Edmonton Oilers' 1980s nucleus of Gretzky–Messier–Anderson–Coffey. Now, all Sid and the kids had to do was live up to the hype. And they got a good start on October 12, 2006, when 19-year-old Crosby scored and 18-year-olds Staal and Kristopher Letang each notched their first NHL goals to pull out a 6–5 win against the New York Rangers. It marked just the ninth time an NHL team has iced a trio of teenage goal scorers in one game, and the first time since teens Dave Andreychuk, Paul Cyr and Phil Housley scored for Buffalo in a 6–4 win against Edmonton on October 17, 1982. Crosby's game-winner, with just 3.3 seconds remaining in regulation time, produced the NHL rarity.

4.10   True

Sports memorabilia hit a new low in 2006, when eBay auctioned a customized McFarlane figurine of Clint Malarchuk's near-fatal skate slash of March 22, 1989. The small, hand-painted ornament depicted the Buffalo goalie crouched over a pool of blood on the ice, clutching his throat to stop the gush from his jugular. Bidding was cut off early—at $40—due to the outcry over bad taste.

4.11 **False**

In his first game with the New York Islanders on March 1, 2007, Ryan Smyth played heads-up hockey after the St. Louis net was accidentally dislodged by linemate Jason Blake during a second-period Islanders attack. Parked at the Blues' crease, with play continuing, Smyth used his skate to inch the post back atop its moorings only a few seconds before Marc-Andre Bergeron's bad-angle shot deflected off a St. Louis player and into the net past Curtis Sanford. The referee had watched the play from behind the cage, ready to whistle "no goal" had the net not been in legal position. (When a net is deliberately dislodged to prevent a goal, the player is penalized under NHL rule 51(c).)

4.12 **True**

Canada's 5–2 victory over the U.S. for the gold medal at the 2002 Winter Olympics was the most-watched television program—sports or otherwise—in the country's history. A third of Canada's entire population, 10.46 million people, were tuned in during the final half-hour of the game, according to Nielsen Research. The entire game averaged 8.7 million viewers, easily topping the 6.7 million who watched the previous record holder, the final game of the 1992 World Series between Toronto and Atlanta.

4.13 False

Talk about capping your expenses. Following the 1999 release of the league's version of Monopoly, in 2006 Hasbro licensed the first NHL team-themed edition of its popular board game to the Minnesota Wild. In the Wild Collector's U.S.$45-edition, franchises cost only $160 and arenas just $900; the prime real estate spaces of Boardwalk and Park Place have been replaced by Jacques Lemaire and his goalie and nephew, Manny Fernandez; the usual game pieces have been substituted with pewter tokens of the Wild logo, hockey skates and, naturally, a Zamboni, and, instead of houses and hotels, there are now warming huts and arenas. Unfortunately, however, Monopoly's famous jail remains a jail—instead of what any puckhead would rightfully argue should be a penalty box.

4.14 True

Daniel Alfredsson became only the second player in NHL history to score the game-winning goal in four consecutive games, when the Senators captain potted the decisive marker in a 5–2 victory over the Washington Capitals on January 16, 2007. (Alfredsson also scored in his next game, versus the Vancouver Canucks, but Roberto Luongo stopped 34 shots in the 2–1 Canucks win.) According to the Elias Sports Bureau, the only NHLer with more consecutive game-winners was Montreal Canadiens forward Newsy Lalonde, who netted five straight in February 1921. Interestingly, it was Lalonde who played—and scored—against the Senators in the first NHL game on December 19, 1917, when the Canadiens triumphed 7–4.

4.15 False

The notion that a player could have the best plus-minus mark in the NHL one year and the worst plus-minus mark in another seems close to impossible. But that's exactly what happened to Paul Ysebaert. In 1991–92, the centre recorded a league-leading plus-44 with the Detroit Red Wings. Six years later, with the last-place Tampa Bay Lightning, Ysebaert posted a league-worst minus-43.

4.16 **True**

Only three players in the Canadiens' storied history have donned No. 33, and if Patrick Roy gets his wish he will be the last. But the goaltender is not holding his breath—at least, not after the way he was run out of town in 1995. Few athletes have been as polarizing as Roy. As a Canadien, he owned league records, a trophy case of hockey's most prized silverware and, perhaps most notable, a major-league attitude that set him on a collision course with rookie coach Mario Tremblay. But Roy's controversial trade to Colorado was probably the best thing that could have happened, at least for Roy, who went on to win two more Cups with the Avalanche and a place for himself in the Hall of Fame. Still, the NHL's winningest goalie places a premium on the Canadiens retiring his No. 33. "I think the Hall of Fame is the crowning moment of a nice career," Roy told the *Gazette*. "I could say it's the cherry on the sundae. But the real cherry for me would be to see my jersey retired with the Canadiens." The Avalanche's No. 33 was retired six months after Roy hung up his pads. Roy's junior team, the Granby Bisons, has also withdrawn its No. 30.

4.17 **False**

If two previous straight shutout losses were not incentive enough, winning one for their coach should have lit the Islanders' fire. Unfortunately, neither provided much motivation, and Ted Nolan's first visit to Buffalo after a nine-year absence was spoiled by a 3–1 loss to the surging Sabres that set a new Islanders scoreless streak, 186:31. Still, Nolan had his club playing better than expected in 2006–07. "It's always nice to come back here," said Nolan, who won NHL coach of the year with Buffalo in 1997 and is one of the most beloved bench bosses in the Sabres' history. Fans cheered, and one sign read: "We wish you well Teddy... just not tonight"—far better treatment than they gave former Sabres forward Miroslav Satan, who was booed every time he touched the puck during the game.

4.18 True

It's a record that won't likely be challenged, given that today's teams play with five-minute overtimes and shootouts to settle tie games. But Philadelphia's 35-game unbeaten streak is still a record-book phenomenon. The Flyers played 85 days and 19 different teams without losing a game between October 14, 1979, and January 7, 1980. Not one team in the league, except Washington, which they never played, could knock the Flyers off their streak of 25 wins and 10 ties. And on December 22 they beat Boston 5–2 and destroyed Montreal's record unbeaten streak of 28 games (22 wins and six ties), set in 1977–78. Among the contenders in the other major league sports, the Flyers also eclipsed the NFL's Canton Bulldogs mark of 25 wins between 1921 and 1923, Major League Baseball's New York Giants streak of 26 in a row in 1916 and the NBA's Los Angeles Lakers run of 33 straight wins in 1971 and 1972.

4.19 True

As of 2006–07, the Lundqvist brothers were only the third set of twins to play against each other and the first ever on opposing teams in forward and goalie positions. "I never see players out there, but I noticed every time *he* was on the ice," Henrik said of his brother, Joel, to the *Associated Press.* "I was nervous every time he was out there, [but] getting the chance to play against him in the NHL is a special feeling." Joel played only 5:44 and failed to register a shot against his twin brother. Henrik made 43 saves in the 5–3 Rangers win against the Stars. Who were the other NHL lookalikes? Rich and Ron Sutter last met up on in March 1994. Patrik and Peter Sundstrom played against each other several times during the 1980s.

4.20 False

Although Penguins goalie Marc-Andre Fleury defeated Philadelphia eight times in 2006–07 (aided by two shootout victories), without suffering a loss or tie, he did not set a new NHL record. The feat was also accomplished by Boston Bruins rookie Frank Brimsek, who logged an 8–0–0 record against Chicago in 1938–39. However, both goalkeepers fall short of Bill Durnan's record. In 1944–45, the Montreal Canadiens goalie posted 10 wins over Boston in 10 games.

4.21 False

In the 1950s, NHL players had little clout when it came to negotiating with management. Witness the example of Gump Worsley. After winning the Calder Trophy as the NHL's top rookie in 1952–53, the New York Rangers netminder figured he was well within his rights to ask for a $500 raise on his $7,500 salary the following fall. His opinion was not shared by Rangers general manager Frank Boucher, however, who demoted Worsley to the Vancouver Canucks of the Western Hockey League and replaced him with American Hockey League veteran goalie Johnny Bower. And, as they did the year before, the club finished out of the playoffs. But the Gumper had a far better time of it out west. The WHL Canucks finished in first place and their netminder was declared both outstanding goaltender and league MVP. And the next fall, Bower played the bulk of the season on the Pacific Coast while Worsley reclaimed his starring role in Manhattan.

4.22 True

Although Curtis Joseph has enjoyed a stellar NHL career, he has not claimed any of the big goalie prizes. Cujo has never been named to an All-Star team, for example, or captured a Vezina Trophy or won the Stanley Cup. Yet, as of 2006–07, Joseph had appeared in 131 playoff games with the Red Wings, Oilers, Maple Leafs and Blues—the most postseason action seen by any goaltender who hasn't raised Lord Stanley's mug.

4.23 True

The claim that announcers get a better sense and feel for the game by being close to the players, coaches and officials at ice level was first tested when the Canadian all-sports network TSN placed Chris Cuthbert and Glenn Healy between the team benches to call the New York Rangers–Buffalo Sabres match on December 1, 2006. With TV numbers hurting (and tanking in the U.S.), broadcasters had begun looking for "unique experiences" in order to sell hockey to dwindling television audiences. Did the experiment work? Cuthbert admitted that "it's pretty special, not perfect," referring to some sightline problems from the low position. Still, the *Globe and Mail* called it a historic success and not just a gimmick, suggesting that that two announcers rinkside did bring viewers closer to the action. TSN also televised games using a one-up, one-down system—a play-by-play man in the booth and an analyst at ice level. And in a November 15 game, colour commentator Pierre McGuire conducted another first by interviewing the Senators' Mike Fisher, who was standing on the ice during a stoppage in play. FSN Detroit was the first U.S. television outlet with play-by-play at ice level. Ken Daniels called the Red Wings–Ottawa Senators game on December 12, 2006. Mickey Redmond stayed in the press box for his game analysis.

4.24 False

After Hockey Canada introduced its change to age classifications for minor hockey, allowing 11-year-old boys to play with 12-year-olds in peewee divisions (where bodychecking is permitted), University of Alberta researchers found that the rate of injuries among the 11-year-olds doubled, while serious injuries, such as concussions and bone fractures, tripled. Data from emergency rooms in the Edmonton region was examined during a four-year period: two years before and two years after the NHL's policy change. Overall, 86 of every 1,000 players aged 11 visited hospital emergency rooms compared to 41 per 1,000 players when no checking was permitted. Across Canada, at least 9,000 hockey players under 16 are treated in hospitals for injuries, and 85 per cent of those injuries are due to bodychecking. The research was published in the July 2006 edition of the *Canadian Medical Association Journal.*

4.25 True

The Rockies didn't accomplish much during their brief six-year NHL stint in Colorado, but they did leave behind one little-known first that went on to become an institution at American sporting events: their theme song, Gary Glitter's glam-rock classic "Rock and Roll" (Part 2). Played when the home team scored or won, the "Hey Song" was dropped from many arena playlists after Glitter's conviction for sexual abuse of a child in 2005. In 2006, the NFL asked teams to stop playing the tune, though several pro clubs had already pulled the sports anthem after the singer was convicted and imprisoned on child pornography charges in 1997.

4.26 True

The new NHL was supposed to be built for scoring. Although goals spiked during the first post-lockout season of 2005–06 (with teams averaging 6.1 goals—the highest average since 1995–96), in 2006–07, goal production dropped to 5.9 on 7,246 goals compared to 7,443 in 2005–06. None of that bothered Martin Brodeur, however, who said after a classic 2–0 goalie duel against the Islanders' Rick DiPietro in December 2006: "People always think a 7–6 game is the way to go for excitement. I think both teams tonight proved that theory wrong." Now, what if Martin Brodeur were NHL commissioner?

4.27 True

Sidney Crosby appears destined to demolish any number of league records, including a few All-Star marks. Crosby, at 19 years and five months of age, is the youngest player voted to an NHL All-Star game since Jaromir Jagr in 1992 at age 19 years and 11 months. Sid the Kid topped all players with 825,783 votes *and* registered the second-highest vote count since balloting to select All-Star starters began in 1986. Jagr received 1,020,736 in 2000.

Drafting Late

WHEN NHL GENERAL MANAGERS and their scouts meet on draft day in search of the next Sidney Crosby or Roberto Luongo, they know the next generation of stars can just as easily come from the late rounds. The selection process after the top five is usually a hit-or-miss venture, one where a highly ranked prospect has every chance of going bust or a deep choice could mature into a Hall of Fame candidate. In this game, match the late draft picks below and their team, draft position and year.

Solutions are on page 121

Pavel Datsyuk	Daniel Alfredsson	Henrik Zetterberg
Eric Daze	Nikolai Khabibulin	Karlis Skrastins
Michael Ryder	Cristobal Huet	Darcy Tucker
Marty Turco	Miikka Kiprusoff	Tomas Kaberle

1. _____Los Angeles (214th in 2001) 2. _____Dallas (124th in 1994)
3. _____Detroit (171st in 1998) 4. _____Montreal (216th in 1998)
5. _____Nashville (230th in 1998) 6. _____Detroit (210th in 1999)
7. _____Toronto (204th in 1996) 8. _____Ottawa (133rd in 1994)
9. _____Montreal (151st in 1993) 10._____San Jose (116th in 1994)
11._____Chicago (90th in 1993) 12._____Winnipeg (204th in 1992)

5

19 Years and 213 Days

WHEN SIDNEY CROSBY WON the NHL scoring race in 2006–07, he became the youngest professional athlete in any North American sport to be crowned a scoring champion. Crosby, who was just 19 years and 213 days old, captured the Art Ross Trophy with 120 points. Wayne Gretzky was 20 years and 88 days old when he won the race in 1980–81. In this chapter, we champion scoring aces and rookie stars.

Answers are on page 74

5.1 In how many consecutive games did Evgeni Malkin score a goal to start his NHL career?

A. Four straight games

B. Five straight games

C. Six straight games

D. Seven straight games

5.2 After Joe Mullen, who was the second U.S.-born player to score 500 NHL goals?

A. Keith Tkachuk

B. Mike Modano

C. Jeremy Roenick

D. John LeClair

5.3 Who is the first player in NHL history—35 years or older—to record consecutive seasons with 40 or more goals?

   A. Teemu Selanne of the Anaheim Ducks

   B. Jaromir Jagr of the New York Rangers

   C. Joe Sakic of the Colorado Avalanche

   D. Ray Whitney of the Carolina Hurricanes

5.4 Who set a rookie point-scoring streak in 2006–07?

   A. Anze Kopitar of the Los Angeles Kings

   B. Paul Stastny of the Colorado Avalanche

   C. Jordan Staal of the Pittsburgh Penguins

   D. Evgeni Malkin of the Pittsburgh Penguins

5.5 After breaking Teemu Selanne's rookie record by scoring a point in 18 straight games, Paul Stastny set a new rookie scoring streak of how long in 2006–07?

   A. An 18-game stretch

   B. A 20-game stretch

   C. A 22-game stretch

   D. A 24-game stretch

5.6 What is the NHL record for the longest point-scoring streak to start an NHL career?

   A. Eight straight games

   B. 10 straight games

   C. 12 straight games

   D. 14 straight games

5.7 After Gordie Howe, which player has the most consecutive 20-goal seasons?

   A. Jaromir Jagr

   B. Brendan Shanahan

C. Mats Sundin

D. Brett Hull

5.8 **Who scored a goal against the most teams in his rookie season?**

A. Alexei Yashin in 1993–94

B. Alexei Kovalev in 1992–93

C. Alexandre Daigle in 1993–94

D. Alexander Ovechkin in 2005–06

5.9 **If the NHL point-streak record is 51 games, what is the American Hockey League mark?**

A. 29 straight games

B. 39 straight games

C. 49 straight games

D. 59 straight games

5.10 **Which rookie in 2006–07 broke Jack Hamilton's 64-year record as the youngest player to score a hat trick?**

A. Jordan Staal of the Pittsburgh Penguins

B. Jiri Hudler of the Detroit Red Wings

C. Evgeni Malkin of the Pittsburgh Penguins

D. Dustin Penner of the Anaheim Ducks

5.11 **With his arm and stick length, what distance does Pittsburgh's Jordan Staal estimate his reach to be from one side of his body to the other?**

A. Six feet

B. Eight feet

C. 10 feet

D. 12 feet

5.12 **What is the NHL record for most power-play goals by a defenseman in a season?**

A. 15 power-play goals

B. 17 power-play goals

C. 19 power-play goals

D. 21 power-play goals

5.13 **Which team duo most recently finished one-two atop the NHL scoring list for defensemen in one season?**

A. Anaheim's Scott Niedermayer and Chris Pronger in 2006–07

B. Detroit's Nicklas Lidstrom and Chris Chelios in 2001–02

C. Calgary's Gary Suter and Al MacInnis in 1987–88

D. Boston's Bobby Orr and Carol Vadnais in 1974–75

5.14 **Who scored three goals in 100 seconds in 2006–07, the second-fastest even-strength hat trick in NHL history?**

A. Ray Whitney of the Carolina Hurricanes

B. Martin Havlat of the Chicago Blackhawks

C. Sidney Crosby of the Pittsburgh Penguins

D. Jonathan Cheechoo of the San Jose Sharks

5.15 **Who is the only player to score 200 career goals without having at least one 20-goal season?**

A. Defenseman Scott Stevens

B. Forward Eric Nesterenko

C. Defenseman Larry Robinson

D. Defenseman Nicklas Lidstrom

5.16 **Which two opposing players produced natural hat tricks in the same game in 2006–07, the first since 1919?**

A. Ryan Smyth and Jonathan Cheechoo

B. Jonathan Cheechoo and Markus Naslund

C. Markus Naslund and Brad Richards

D. Brad Richards and Ryan Smyth

5.17 **What is the individual record for scoring goals in the most consecutive regular-season games against the same opponent?**

A. Six consecutive games

B. Seven consecutive games

C. Eight consecutive games

D. Nine consecutive games

5.18 **Who is the youngest player to reach 200 career points?**

A. Wayne Gretzky

B. Peter Stastny

C. Mario Lemieux

D. Sidney Crosby

19 Years and 213 Days

Answers

5.1 **C. Six straight games**

Few rookies skate into the NHL record books after just six career games. For most, an NHL start is a kick-the-tires foray for their team followed by a one-way ticket back to the minors. And even fewer, if they are successful at the NHL level, ever get mentioned in the same breath as Hall of Famers Joe Malone, Newsy Lalonde or Cy Denneny. Yet that's what Evgeni Malkin accomplished in 2006–07—or, more precisely, what he did between October 18 and November 1, 2006, when the 20-year-old Russian popped a goal in each of his first six games to become the first player since Malone, Lalonde and Denneny scored in their first six matches 89 years earlier during the NHL's inaugural season of 1917–18. In fact, Malkin should own the record outright. No criticism intended, but Malone, Lalonde and Denneny weren't true rookies, considering they already had established playing careers when the league opened for business. Malone was 27 years old, Lalonde, 29, and Denneny, 25, in 1917–18. Note: Malone holds the all-time freshman record, after scoring goals in his first 14 games. Among modern players, Malkin's six topped Dmitri Kvartalnov's run of five for Boston in 1992–93.

5.2   B. Mike Modano

Mike Modano became the second American-born NHLer to score 500 regular-season goals in a 3–2 win against Philadelphia on March 13, 2007. Oddly enough, it happened exactly 10 years minus one day after Mullen notched his 500th on March 14, 1997, against Patrick Roy in Colorado. Modano's milestone marker put him only two behind Mullen's all-time tally of 502, the highest total by a U.S.-born player. Four nights later, Mullen finally relinquished his title to Modano when the 36-year-old native of Livonia, Michigan, set a new NHL mark for Americans with his 502nd and 503rd goals on March 17 in a 3–2 loss to Nashville. But no one was happier for Modano than Mullen, who said, "It couldn't happen to a better hockey player and a better guy. He's a great role model for the kids." Mullen should know. His own playing career, which inspired inner-city kids in New York to see a future in the game, was later duplicated by Modano. When the Stars moved to Dallas, there were only three hockey rinks in northern Texas and no high-school programs. But today Dallas is a hockey playground, with 23 sheets of ice for more than 7,500 young players and 70 high-school teams.

5.3 A. Teemu Selanne of the Anaheim Ducks

Father Time has nothing on Teemu Selanne. A number of veterans faced early retirement and some quit after the players lockout of 2004–05, but Selanne came back rejuvenated—with more power and speed and a pain-free knee. In fact, he signed as a free agent with Anaheim in 2005 and potted 40 goals, his first big offensive season since 1998–99. Then, in 2006–07, the 36-year-old delivered another plus-40-goal year, and amassed 48 goals to become the first NHLer over the age of 35 to notch back-to-back 40-goal seasons. It was Selanne's seventh season of 40 or more goals.

5.4 B. Paul Stastny of the Colorado Avalanche

Anyone watching Paul Stastny in 2006–07 could see why the strapping 21-year-old centre was making the rookie-of-the-year race tight for his rivals, Evgeni Malkin and Jordan Stall. Stastny "plays well beyond his years," Colorado captain Joe Sakic remarked during the freshman's 18-game point-scoring streak, the longest on NHL record by a rookie. But Stastny's natural feel for the action may have something to do with his gene pool—after all, he is the son of superstar Peter Stastny, the league's most prolific scorer after Wayne Gretzky in the 1980s. "He's got a hockey sense that you can't teach," Avalanche coach Joel Quenneville commented during Stastny's stellar year. Stastny, who wears his father's No. 26, earned the rookie record after assisting on a Milan Hejduk goal on March 11. (The previous mark of 17 games was set by Teemu Selanne in 1992–93.) During his stretch, which began on February 3, Stastny scored eight goals and 18 assists with a plus-10—beating his father's franchise record of one point or more in 16 straight games. Stastny Sr.'s streak included 15 consecutive road games with a point, January 13 to March 17— a new rookie record that busted the league's 13-game mark held by his uncle, Marion Stastny, in 1981–82. Oh yeah, the bloodlines are there.

5.5   B. A 20-game stretch

After smashing Teemu Selanne's NHL mark of 17 to set the new rookie run at 18 games of one point or more, Paul Stastny bumped the count to 20 matches—giving pause to any future freshman with plans of erasing the Stastny name from the NHL record books. During his February 3 to March 17 streak, the red-hot Stastny—with 11 goals and 18 assists with a plus-12 rating—shot into contention for the coveted Calder Trophy and led Colorado in its playoff bid to within one point of contention. The scoring drive made the 21-year-old the third-youngest player in league annals to notch a 20-game point streak, at 21 years and 80 days old, compared to league leaders Mario Lemieux (who was 20 years and 161 days old on the last day of his 28-game streak in 1985–86) and Wayne Gretzky (who was 21 years and 36 days old on the last day of his 24-game streak in 1981–82).

5.6   D. 14 straight games

There's no official NHL record for point-scoring streaks by rookies. And that's unfortunate, because more fans should know of Dmitri Kvartalnov, or, more specifically, what he pulled off as a freshman with Boston in 1992–93. Kvartalnov enjoyed a long career in Europe, including appearances with the USSR national team at the 1989 and 1991 World

Championships, yet, by NHL standards, he was a flash-in-the-pan, his rise to prominence as swift as his sudden departure as a 112-game player who scored 42 goals and 91 points in just two seasons with the Bruins. Still, Kvartalnov's stellar start included a remarkable 14-game point-scoring streak that jump-started his NHL career and earned the 26-year-old rookie 12 goals and 22 points between October 8 and November 12, 1992. As well, as mentioned in question 5.1, he scored an unprecedented five of those goals in his first five games, a feat topped only by Evgeni Malkin's six in 2006–07.

5.7   B. Brendan Shanahan

Several big names—bigger than Brendan Shanahan's—have challenged Gordie Howe and his monster record of 22 consecutive seasons of 20 or more goals. Marcel Dionne and Brett Hull got to 17 straight seasons. Ron Francis totalled 20, but tripped up midway with an 11-goal year during the condensed 48-game schedule of 1994–95's player lockout. And Dave Andreychuk's career included 19 20-goal seasons interrupted by two defensive-oriented seasons in New Jersey. Only Shanahan has been a model of consistency, notching his 18th straight year of 20 or more goals in 2006–07. So does the ageing sniper have the longevity for a shot at Howe's famous mark? Shanahan will have to play until he is 42 to find out.

5.8   D. Alexander Ovechkin in 2005–06

Playing in a 30-team NHL might be an unfair advantage to any rookie trying to top Teemu Selanne's record of goal scoring against 21 teams in a season. But with the league's unbalanced schedule, teams in 2005–06 played against 24 clubs, or only one more than the number Selanne faced as a freshman in

1992–93's 24-team league. And that one extra opponent could make the difference. Alexander Ovechkin beat Selanne's 21 count and recorded goals against 22 of Washington's 24 opponents in 2005–06—the most teams any rookie has ever scored upon. In fact, Ovechkin totalled 52 of the Capitals' 230 goals for an NHL-best 22.6 per cent—scoring against every team the Capitals challenged (except San Jose and Los Angeles).

5.9   B. 39 straight games

The longest point-scoring streak in the AHL's 71-year history belongs to Chicago Wolves right wing Darren Haydar, who set a new mark of 32 straight games with a goal and assist in a 2–1 win over San Antonio on December 23, 2006. After eclipsing the 31-game record Binghamton's Mike Richard set in 1987–88, Haydar, an Atlanta Thrashers free agent in 2006, extended his minor-league streak to 39, scoring 24 goals and 80 points between October 7, 2006, and January 6, 2007.

5.10   A. Jordan Staal of the Pittsburgh Penguins

His teammates nicknamed him Gronk, after a comic book character. Apparently, Jordan Staal's huge size—six foot four—makes him scary, which is how many already felt about his rookie campaign in 2006–07, when he set an unprecedented number of "youngest" records in penalty shots and shorthanded goals. Then, on February 10 against Toronto, Staal notched the game's first two goals and the overtime winner in the Penguins' 6–5 victory to become the youngest player ever to score a hat trick. He was just 18 years and 153 days old—more than a month younger than Jack Hamilton, who was 18 years and 185 days old when he scored four times against the Rangers on December 4, 1943.

5.11   C. 10 feet

When 2006–07 began, Pittsburgh had no big expectations of Jordan Staal. They figured on playing him for a maximum of nine games before returning him to the OHL Peterborough Petes, enough time for the Penguins to test drive their 2006 first-rounder while preventing the first year of his three-year entry-level contract from kicking in. However, Staal played so

Jordan Staal's Rookie Records of 2006–07

DATE	OPPONENT	ACHIEVEMENT	AGE
Oct. 21	Columbus	Two Shorthand Goals	18 years, 41 days

- Youngest player with two SH goals in a single game, including penalty shot goal
  (Surpassed Radek Dvorak: 20 years, 278 days)
- Only player to score more than one SH goal before his 19th birthday
- Youngest player to score two goals in a single game in 63 years
  (Previously Bep Guidolin: 18 years, 12 days)
- Youngest player to score on penalty shot
  (Surpassed Nathan Horton: 18 years, 224 days)

DATE	OPPONENT	ACHIEVEMENT	AGE
Nov. 25	NYR	Overtime Penalty Shot	18 years, 76 days

- First rookie with OT penalty shot since league adopted rule in 1983–84
- Tied several rookies with most penalty shots (2) in one season
  (Only David Vyborny has two PS goals, 2000–01)

DATE	OPPONENT	ACHIEVEMENT	AGE
Mar. 6	Ottawa	Seventh Shorthand Goal	18 years, 177 days

- Set rookie record with his seventh SH goal
  (Surpassed Gerry Minor and John Madden: six SH goals)

well that he jumped to the Penguins' second line, just four months after draft day. The 18-year-old played anything but like a teenager, and, within a month, proved just how much the NHL was now a young man's game. No, Pittsburgh never figured on Staal for 2006–07. Nor did many netminders. His success came in part from being able to get a shot off with the puck far from his body. Staal figures he has a wingspan that can sweep the puck from one side of his body to the other by as much as 10 feet. "I think it kind of fools goalies when I have it stretched out and I just let it go. They're not expecting a shot," the six-four Staal has said.

5.12 C. 19 power-play goals

For all of his weaknesses on the blueline, including easily being beat one-on-one and taking bad penalties, Sheldon Souray turned around his image as a lumbering rearguard in the speedy NHL with a career year in 2006–07. Leading Montreal to a league-high 22.8 per cent success rate on 86 goals in 378 opportunities, Souray's laser beam slap shots set a new NHL mark among defensemen—with 19 goals on the man-advantage. His record-setting 19th came against the Rangers' Henrik Lundqvist in a 3–1 loss on April 5. The previous league mark of 18 power-play goals was set by the Islanders' Denis Potvin in 1975–76 and matched by Adrian Aucoin of Vancouver in 1998–99. In 1985–86, forward Tim Kerr set the all-time record at 34 goals.

5.13 C. Calgary's Gary Suter and Al MacInnis in 1987–88

Since 1967–68, only two pairs of rearguards from the same team have led all defensemen in scoring. The New York Islanders iced the Potvin brothers in 1975–76, with Denis collecting 98 points and Jean earning 72, certainly a league first for siblings. Despite the pairings of such high-profile blueline stars as Lidstrom–Chelios, Niedermayer–Pronger and Orr–Vadnais, the most recent defensive duo with a one-two league finish is Gary Suter (91 points) and Al MacInnis (83) with the first-place Calgary Flames in 1987–88.

5.14   A. Ray Whitney of the Carolina Hurricanes

Call it the Ray Whitney magic trick. In the second period of a road game against the Boston Bruins on February 8, 2007, the Hurricanes winger exploded for three goals in a span of 100 seconds. Whitney scored his first marker at 15:36, his second at 16:45 and his third at 17:16, giving the 'Canes a 3–1 lead. But his third goal was greeted by a lone hat and cascade of boos. "Things happen quick in this game," Bruins coach Dave Lewis said afterwards, "but normally, you don't want them to happen that quick." By the time second intermission rolled around, Whitney had also picked up an assist on Justin Williams's power-play goal. He then added another assist on Rod Brind'Amour's empty-netter in the third period to cap a five-point night in Carolina's 5–2 win. And, though Whitney's hat trick was well short of league record leader Bill Mosienko's 21-second hat trick, it comfortably beat the Whalers–Hurricanes franchise mark held by Ron Francis, who scored a hat trick in a span of 8:05 in 1985. Remarkably, it was only the second hat trick of Whitney's 15-year career.

5.15   C. Defenseman Larry Robinson

It is not easy to score 200 career goals without having at least one 20-goal season. Yet, as of 2006–07, only one player has ever managed the feat—Larry Robinson. The Big Bird compiled 208 career goals in his 20-year career and got agonizingly close to the 20-goal plateau on two other occasions (when he netted

19 goals for Montreal in 1976–77 and 1985–86). Comparatively, Scott Stevens totalled 196 career goals and had one 21-goal season; Eric Nesterenko played 21 seasons and scored 250 times, yet only registered one 20-goal year (1957–58); and Nicklas Lidstrom passed the 200-goal mark in 2006–07, recording a career-high 20 goals in 1999–2000.

5.16   A. Ryan Smyth and Jonathan Cheechoo

The NHL should have proclaimed October 12, 2006, official hat trick night. Between two games an unusually high number of natural hat tricks were tallied—three in all. First, the Devils' Brian Gionta scored three straight in a comeback win against Toronto; then, Ryan Smyth matched Jonathan Cheechoo's hat trick to help Edmonton erase a 4–1 deficit and earn a stunning 6–4 victory against San Jose. It was the first time in 87 years and only the second time ever that opposing players scored naturals in a single game. (Montreal's Didier Pitre and Ottawa's Jack Darragh each had natural hat tricks in the Canadiens' 10–6 win on January 16, 1919.) Smyth notched his three in an Oilers-record 2:01 on two deflections and a rebound, causing teammate Ethan Moreau to joke: "He scored three goals in 2:01, and the puck was on his stick for a total of four-tenths of a second. That's vintage Smitty." Smyth broke Wayne Gretzky's team mark of 2:18.

5.17   C. Eight consecutive games

Mike Knuble certainly enjoys playing against Buffalo. The right-winger scored goals against the Sabres in eight consecutive regular-season games to set an NHL record. The first four goals came when Knuble was with the Boston Bruins in 2003–04. The second four came in 2005–06, the year after the lockout, when he was a member of the Philadelphia Flyers. In the first round of the 2006 playoffs, Knuble then scored his ninth straight goal against Buffalo in the first game of their 2006 playoff series, but was blanked in the next five games as Buffalo took the series. His regular-season streak against the Sabres was snapped when Buffalo crushed the Flyers 9–1 in their first meeting in 2006–07. Knuble also has a few record chasers, including Alex Ovechkin, who scored in seven straight games against Philadelphia as of 2006–07.

5.18 D. Sidney Crosby

The sophomore season of Sidney Crosby proved to be his defining year as an elite athlete. In 2006–07, he confirmed that his spectacular rookie season was no fluke. In fact, Crosby bypassed superstar status to become the future of NHL hockey. After scoring his first six-point game on December 13, 2006, he took over the scoring lead—the first teenager to do so since Wayne Gretzky in 1979–80. Even more Gretzky-like was Crosby's goal against Carolina's Cam Ward on March 2, which made Crosby the youngest player in league history to record 200 career points. And he achieved the milestone at the age of 19 years and 207 days—more than three months earlier than Wayne Gretzky's 200th, which came at 19 years and 347 days. Then, on March 10, Crosby scored his 100th point of 2006–07 to become the youngest player and just the fifth player in NHL history to reach 100-point seasons in each of his first two seasons, a feat only Gretzky, Mario Lemieux, Mike Rogers and Peter Stastny have also accomplished.

History Highlights

ON **APRIL 18, 2006,** the NHL played its last 10 games of 2005–06, and, though playoff positions had been mostly decided, the league witnessed an important first. Alexander Ovechkin's final four shots on goal against Tampa Bay brought his season's total to 425, a rookie record. It was also the first time a freshman ever led the league in shots. So you still think after Game 1 you're a hockey historian? Try these.

Solutions are on page 122

March 21, 1985	December 8, 1987	March 17, 1955
June 5, 1991	October 3, 1953	February 24, 1982
March 12, 1980	February 2, 1977	November 12, 1942
March 24–25, 1936		

1. _____Brett Hull duplicated his father Bobby's MVP Hart Trophy.
2. _____Mud Bruneteau scored to end the NHL's longest game.
3. _____The Howes became the first father–son linemates in NHL play.
4. _____The Richard Riot: Montreal fans went on a rampage through downtown.
5. _____Ian Turnbull set a defenseman record with his five-goal game.
6. _____Bobby Carpenter became the first American-born 50-goal scorer.
7. _____Ron Hextall became first NHL goalie to shoot and score a goal.
8. _____Bep Guidolin played his first game as NHL's youngest player.
9. _____Jean Béliveau left semi-pro hockey to finally sign with Montreal.
10._____Wayne Gretzky scored his 50th goal in his record-setting 39th game.

6

Team Dad

THE FIRST TEAM TO INVITE the fathers of players on a road trip was probably the Nashville Predators. They asked players' dads to accompany their sons during the franchise's inaugural season in 1998–99, and have held their annual "Dads' Trip" ever since, including a father-son outing in 2006–07 when 23 fathers made a two-game road trip to Philadelphia and St. Louis. Since then, Minnesota, Pittsburgh and the Islanders have all rewarded NHL fathers for their sacrifices in chasing their sons' dreams. (Moms have often played larger roles, but it would be "kind of weird" bringing them along, according to the Wild's Mark Parrish.) In this chapter, we focus on teams with family spirit.

Answers are on page 91

6.1 **Before Sidney Crosby and Evgeni Malkin did it with Pittsburgh in 2006–07, which NHL team tandem last won the league and rookie scoring races in the same season?**

A. It had never happened before

B. The NY Islanders' Bryan Trottier and Mike Bossy

C. Montreal's Bernie Geoffrion and Bobby Rousseau

D. Chicago's Bobby Hull and Billy Hay

6.2 How many consecutive games did Edmonton lose after dealing captain Ryan Smyth to the New York Islanders in February 2007?

A. None, the Oilers won their first game without Ryan Smyth

B. Three straight losses

C. Five straight losses

D. Eight straight losses

6.3 In 2006–07, which team's Zamboni drivers were accused of making bad ice for shootouts at the opponent's end of the rink?

A. The Montreal Canadiens

B. The Boston Bruins

C. The Edmonton Oilers

D. The Vancouver Canucks

6.4 What is the NHL team record for most consecutive games without going into overtime?

A. 29 straight games

B. 49 straight games

C. 69 straight games

D. 89 straight games

6.5 How many times did the New Jersey Devils score a goal after pulling their goaltender for an extra attacker 23 times in 2006–07?

A. Four times

B. Eight times

C. 12 times

D. 16 times

6.6 What NHL first occurred at the game between the Chicago Blackhawks and the Toronto Maple Leafs on December 2, 1950?

A. There was not a single penalty called

B. The game was delayed by a bomb threat

C. Three goalies were picked as the three stars

D. The two opposing coaches engaged in a fist fight

6.7 Which modern-era NHL team has been blanked the most times in a season since the record was set in 1928–29?

A. The Washington Capitals in 1974–75

B. The Ottawa Senators in 1992–93

C. The San Jose Sharks in 1992–93

D. The Columbus Blue Jackets in 2006–07

6.8 Which two teams have played the most regular-season games against one another in NHL history?

A. The Montreal Canadiens and the Boston Bruins

B. The Chicago Blackhawks and the Detroit Red Wings

C. The New York Rangers and the Boston Bruins

D. The Toronto Maple Leafs and the Montreal Canadiens

6.9 In 2006–07, which NHL team set a new North American record for most fans wearing wigs at a sporting event?

A. The San Jose Sharks

B. The Calgary Flames

C. The St. Louis Blues

D. The Philadelphia Flyers

6.10 How many wins did the Buffalo Sabres register in 2006–07 to tie the NHL record for most victories from the start of a season?

A. Six straight wins

B. Eight straight wins

C. 10 straight wins

D. 12 straight wins

6.11 Which NHL team had its 66-year-old record of best road start in a season destroyed by the Buffalo Sabres in 2006–07?

A. The Toronto Maple Leafs

B. The Boston Bruins

C. The Detroit Red Wings

D. The New York Americans

6.12 Which team was the first to regularly play "The Hockey Song," by Stompin' Tom Connors, during its home games?

A. The Ottawa Senators

B. The Vancouver Canucks

C. The Edmonton Oilers

D. The Toronto Maple Leafs

6.13 In Anaheim's NHL record-setting 16-game unbeaten streak at the start of 2006–07, how many games did the Ducks actually lose?

A. None

B. One game

C. Two games

D. Four games

6.14 What is the NHL record for most points by a team in 15 games on the road?

A. 18 team points

B. 22 team points

C. 26 team points

D. 30 team points

6.15 Which NHL team made history in 2004 by officially adopting a mascot from Major League Baseball?

A. The Montreal Canadiens

B. The Atlanta Thrashers

C. The Pittsburgh Penguins

D. The Los Angeles Kings

6.16 What is the record for longest winning streak on the road in one season by a team?

A. 10 road games

B. 12 road games

C. 14 road games

D. 16 road games

6.17 In January 2007, which NHL team introduced "the Lay's Fan Zam," a custom-modified Zamboni designed for entertaining, rather than ice cleaning?

A. The Nashville Predators

B. The Florida Panthers

C. The Dallas Stars

D. The San Jose Sharks

6.18 How many games did Pittsburgh lose in a row when Sidney Crosby was held without a point during his first two seasons?

A. None, Pittsburgh won its first game with Crosby scoreless

B. 10 consecutive losses

C. 20 consecutive losses

D. 30 consecutive losses

6.19 Which club's record streak of 487 consecutive home sell-outs came to an end in 2006–07?

A. The Edmonton Oilers'

B. The Colorado Avalanche's

C. The Toronto Maple Leafs'

D. The Detroit Red Wings'

6.20 What is the most number of regular-season games played by a franchise before its first playoff match?

A. Less than 300 games

B. Between 300 and 500 games

C. Between 500 and 700 games

D. More than 700 games

Team Dad

Answers

6.1 **D. Chicago's Bobby Hull and Billy Hay**

With top-five picks in five successive drafts between 2002 and 2006, Pittsburgh finally had its breakout year in 2006–07. The Penguins' kiddie corps rocked the league with a slew of firsts, mosts and youngest records, including scoring titles by Sidney Crosby and rookie Evgeni Malkin. Crosby, the youngest scoring champion in NHL history, led all scorers with 120 points; Malkin topped all freshman, compiling 85 points. The last team to capture both scoring titles was the Chicago Blackhawks in 1959–60, when Bobby Hull won the Art Ross Trophy with 81 points and Billy Hay was best among first-year players with 55 points. Only seven other teams in league history have boasted rosters with duo scoring champs in one year. The Montreal Maroons remain the lone team to sport a rookie who led all players in scoring. Nels Stewart, who joined the NHL at age 22, won the scoring title with 42 points in 36 games during 1925–26.

6.2   D. Eight straight losses

After trading away its heart and soul to the Islanders at the 2007 trading deadline on February 27, Edmonton dropped the next eight games to match the second-longest losing streak in franchise history. During the skid, which didn't include the team's first loss in Ryan Smyth's last game as an Oiler, Edmonton was outscored 30–6, one of the worst offensive droughts by any club in an eight-game span in a half-century of hockey. Injuries or the flu sidelined 11 regulars and added to Edmonton's woes, but it was Smyth's departure that proved gut-wrenching—and predictable. For that reason, the Oilers almost caved to Smyth's not-a-penny-less-than-U.S.$27.5-million demand, but chose instead to continue to rebuild with a strong crop of young talents, draft picks and prospects—an unlikely scenario for a team that, only nine months earlier, had lost the 2006 Stanley Cup by just one win. Only an overtime loss (where the team earned a point) in their ninth game without Smyth, on March 17 to St. Louis, spared Edmonton from matching the club record of 11 straight losses. Including that overtime loss, the Oilers went on a 12-game winless streak, recording their first victory on March 23, almost a month after trading their spiritual leader. Meanwhile, during that same period with his new team, Smyth scored 12 points, or about the same point average during his 10-year career in Edmonton, and the Islanders squeaked into the 2007 playoffs with their deadline acquisition.

6.3   A. The Montreal Canadiens

In what might be the most brazen act of mischief by ice-makers since Trent Evans buried a Canadian dollar coin under centre ice at the 2002 Olympics, Zamboni drivers at Montreal's Bell Centre provided a little hometown edge to the Canadiens by clearing a narrower lane in the opposition's shooting zone for a shootout against the Toronto Maple Leafs on December 2, 2006. Pointing the finger was Toronto coach Paul Maurice, whose demand for an additional ice-scraping job to widen the path for his shooters was rejected by the referees. But upon video review, NHL official Mike Murphy said the swath of cleaned ice from the blueline to the crease of Cristobal Huet did look "narrower." It was the second time that Maurice accused Montreal's Zamboni drivers of hindering his scorers during a shootout. In the first instance, on October 28, the Maple Leafs took the extra point. But on December 2, Toronto lost when Huet gave up one goal to Mats Sundin while Saku Koivu and Sheldon Souray connected for the Canadiens. The final score? Montreal and its Zamboni cheats: 4, Toronto: 3.

6.4   B. 49 straight games

The San Jose Sharks detest overtimes, but they hate shootouts even more. The Sharks finished 30th among the NHL's 30 teams with an awful 1–7 shootout record in 2005–06. In OT, the Sharks had a very respectable 9–4, but, then again, overtime often leads to the dreaded shootout. So San Jose played a once-bitten-twice-shy game in regulation in 2006–07, and went 49 matches without an extra period from October 6 to January 30, the longest streak since the five-minute overtime rule was introduced in 1983–84.

6.5   B. Eight times

How often does a team yank its goalie for an extra attacker and the strategy pays off in a goal? Not that often, except for the New Jersey Devils in 2006–07, when they pulled Martin Brodeur and Scott Clemmensen 23 times to gain the man-advantage with the clock ticking down. On 15 occasions the manoeuvre failed to produce a goal, and six other times it backfired, giving the opposition an empty-netter. But in eight other contests—a possible league record—the Devils scored, six times forcing the extra session. New Jersey went on to win just three of those six matches, one in overtime and two in the shootout. Brian Gionta might just be the poster boy for the extra-attacker tactic. He managed an unusual league record by scoring four goals on October 12 and 19 and December 12 and January 20, with the Devils' net empty in the dying moments. Zach Parise had two, on February 1 and March 28, and Sergei Brylin and John Madden, on March 2 and April 8, respectively, each had one last-ditch marker.

6.6   C. Three goalies were picked as the three stars

Being a goalie in the days before the advent of the mask was a hazardous job, a fact never more evident than during the game between Chicago and Toronto at Maple Leaf Gardens on December 2, 1950. In the second period, a shot struck Toronto goalie Al Rollins above the left eye, and he had to be carried off the ice on a stretcher. He was replaced by backup Turk Broda, who had been watching the game from the stands. A few minutes later, Chicago goalie Harry Lumley was struck in the face by a deflected puck and left the ice to undergo repairs. Then, during the third period, Lumley went to the Chicago bench to receive medical aid, and, during the delay, the crowd began to boo—until it was announced that Lumley was playing with a broken nose. The game ended in a scoreless draw, and the three stars were announced as Lumley, Broda and Rollins, three goalies—an NHL first.

6.7   D. The Columbus Blue Jackets in 2006–07

One of hockey's most embarrassing and, apparently, safest team records belongs to the Chicago Blackhawks. Going on 80 years, the Hawks still lead the NHL in most games blanked in a season after humiliating themselves with 20 zeroes in the 44-game schedule of 1928–29. (In that era, before the introduction of the redline and without forward passing in the offensive zone, shutouts were commonplace. The Pittsburgh Pirates suffered a similar fate that same season with 18 zeroes.) But the Blackhawks' one-off record should not be taken lightly, as Columbus found out in 2006–07, when it courted humiliation with 16 zeroes by opposing teams. It set a modern record, surpassing the 14 shutout defeats of Pittsburgh in 1969–70 and Minnesota in 2000–01. Note: The 1928–29 Hawks own a few other train-wreck records that the Blue Jackets should also stay clear of, including most consecutive games shutout (8), fewest goals in a season (33) and lowest goals-per-game average (0.75). Chicago finished 1928–29 with a 7-29-8 record; Columbus had a 33-42-7 mark in 2006–07.

6.8 B. The Chicago Blackhawks and the Detroit Red Wings

Considering that Montreal and Toronto were both members of the NHL when the league was created in 1917, one might logically assume they would have played more games against one another than any other pair of teams. But that's not the case. Entering the 2007–08 season, Chicago and Detroit had met 689 times—10 more times than Montreal and Toronto. And even though the Blackhawks and the Red Wings did not join the league until 1926, they have overtaken Montreal and Toronto because of unbalanced schedules and increased inter-division play in recent years.

6.9 D. The Philadelphia Flyers

The Flyers had a dismal season in 2006–07, but they did create a buzz of excitement on October 30, 2006, when fans were given bright-orange wigs by the team for a game against the Chicago Blackhawks at the Wachovia Center. The hairy handouts were part of an effort to break the *Guinness World Records* stat for "most fans wearing wigs—single venue." The Flyers unofficially broke the old record of 6,213 fans at a Detroit Pistons game on March 19, 2004, by gathering 9,315 signatures from the 18,876 fans attending the game.

6.10 C. 10 straight wins

It's a good thing that Buffalo didn't have to play Toronto before it recorded its 10th consecutive win from the start of 2006–07. Otherwise, the Maple Leafs might have halted the Sabres' streak early, considering the Leafs' cherished 1993–94 record of 10 straight victories was on the line. Still, at the first opportunity—in Buffalo's 13th game—the Leafs took revenge, handing the Sabres their first defeat in regulation, a 4–1 setback on November 4, 2006. And in the end, Buffalo only tied

Toronto's record 10-win streak after the Sabres' 11th game ended in a 5-4 shootout loss to Atlanta. "I'm a little ticked off," said Sabres goalie Ryan Miller. "It would have been fun to be on our own; a little piece of history...."

6.11   A. The Toronto Maple Leafs

While Buffalo had to settle for sharing the NHL's longest winning streak from start of season with Toronto (see our previous answer), the Sabres took some solace in establishing a new league mark for the best road start in 2006–07. The team demolished the Maple Leafs' long-standing run of seven road wins to start 1940–41 with a record-setting road-win streak of 10 victories between October 4 and November 13, 2006. Since 1940, only the 1985–86 Philadelphia Flyers and 2005–06 Detroit Red Wings managed to tie Toronto's mark.

6.12   A. The Ottawa Senators

"The Hockey Song," written and made famous by Stompin' Tom Connors, is often sung at hockey arenas—both large and small venues. The song, which is split into three verses, each describing a period of play in a typical game, is well-known for its catchy chorus: "Oh, the good old hockey game, is the best game you can name. And the best game you can name, is the good old hockey game!" The song first appeared on Connors's 1973 album, "Stompin Tom and the Hockey Song," but the tune did not attain major popularity until 1992, when the Ottawa Senators began playing it at their games. Fans quickly took a liking to the song and it spread throughout the NHL.

6.13   D. Four games

When is a loss not *really* a loss? Only in an NHL game, where the league can suspend reality by ignoring the final score and award one point to the losing team. Of course, this doesn't happen in regulation time; though it does in an overtime or shootout situation. But Anaheim isn't complaining, not since it entered the record books with the longest unbeaten streak to start a season. The Ducks topped the league's previous best 15-game start (12–0–3, by Edmonton in 1984–85) with a 12–0–4 record between October 6 and November 9, 2007. But in those first 16 contests, the Ducks suffered three shootout losses, which the NHL didn't have in 1984–85, and one overtime defeat in their 13th game, a guaranteed streak-breaker during the Oilers' run. Anaheim also collected a league-high 28 points—the record for most points without a loss at the start of a season, if you believe reality, NHL style.

6.14   C. 26 team points

The best road record through 15 games in NHL history belongs to the Anaheim Ducks, who amassed a 12–1–2 record for 26 points away from home between October 7 and December 13, 2006. Anaheim's four shootout matches in those 15 games were crucial to its new league mark. The Ducks won two and lost two, but still netted six team points. (Without shootouts in their era, the 1951–52 Detroit Red Wings scored 25 points on a 10–0–5 record between October 18 and December 20.) Anaheim came back to earth after their first-half season surge to finish with a 22–14–5 road record in 2006–07.

6.15   A. The Montreal Canadiens

When the Montreal Expos baseball team moved to Washington D.C. to become the Nationals in 2004, they left behind a lot of broken hearts among the fans of Nos Amours (the French nickname for the team, which means "Our Loves"). Of course, Youppi!, the club's furry, orange mascot, was also left behind—but not without a home. In September 2004, the Canadiens adopted Youppi! as their official mascot, the first in the team's 90-plus-year history. And with the switch, Youppi! became the first mascot in professional sports to switch leagues. "When we had the opportunity to preserve a small element of the Montreal Expos legacy, there was no hesitation on our part to do so," said Canadiens executive Ray Lalonde, though not everyone applauded the move. Some hockey purists regard Youppi!'s comical gyrations in the aisles of the Bell Centre, much like the blaring music and Jumbotron graphics, as just one more needless distraction.

6.16 B. 12 road games

The advent of regular-season overtime and the shootout has changed the title holders of many NHL records. This may not be an across-the-board phenomenon, but check out the leaders for the longest winning streak on the road in one season. Before overtime in 1983–84, the best road run was eight games (held by five teams, all equalling the mark between 1971–72 and 1981–82). While in the first season of overtime, 1983–84, Buffalo set a new record of 10 successive wins on the road between December 10 and January 23, 1984. Surprisingly, none of those Sabres victories were overtime decisions, but all the other leaders—St. Louis, with 10 straight road wins in 1999–2000, New Jersey, with 10 in 2000–01, and Buffalo, with nine in 2005–06—sustained their streaks with at least one overtime or shootout win. One argument is that the teams still had to win those road games, but, it was with an advantage not available to previous record holders. Currently, the Detroit Red Wings lead this category with 12 successive victories away between March 1 and April 15, 2006. The Red Wings did it with two shootout victories.

6.17 C. The Dallas Stars

The Stars' new addition to the NHL's endless parade of marketing gimmicks made its debut at American Airlines Center during the second intermission of a game against the Pittsburgh Penguins on January 27, 2007. The Lay's Fan Zam does not clean ice (the on-board water tank normally used to flood the rink's surface was removed to create a seating area for up to 10 people)—instead, its sole purpose is to entertain. The pimped-up Zamboni is fitted with a 110-cubic-inch Harley Davidson engine, 24-inch chrome rims and a chrome steering wheel, and features a sound system with seven 1200-watt amplifiers, strobes and neon lights, hydraulics, a smoke machine and three XBOX 360 systems with individual 19-inch monitors. It is also equipped with hockey-stick-shaped exhaust pipes and its front grille boasts an operating 52-inch plasma television. At each home game, fans register to take a ride in the flashy vehicle, and, presumably, acquire a craving for potato chips.

6.18 D. 30 consecutive losses

As Sid the Kid goes, so does Pittsburgh. During Crosby's first two seasons, the Penguins were a brutal 6–34–1 in games when the young star was held pointless. In fact, the team didn't win a match when Crosby's linescore was all zeroes until a 2–0 victory against Washington on February 3, 2007. It was Crosby's 31st game without a point. "It's not too often Sid doesn't get a point, but when he does, it's good that other players step up and take the game under control," said teammate Jordan Staal.

6.19   B. The Colorado Avalanche's

Some doubted that Denver could support an NHL franchise
when the Quebec Nordiques relocated to the mile-high city
in 1995–96. The NHL's Colorado Rockies didn't draw well in
their six-season run before the franchise moved to New Jersey
in 1982, and the World Hockey Association Denver Spurs
lasted less than a season prior to their departure for Ottawa.
But Denver fans responded to the Avalanche, which won the
Stanley Cup its first year in town, and the team was soon sell-
ing out on a nightly basis. Their home sellout streak began on
November 9, 1995, and lasted until October 16, 2007, when the
Avalanche hosted Chicago. The official attendance of 17,681
was 326 seats short of capacity in the Pepsi Center, ending the
longest recorded sellout streak in NHL history, at 487 games.

6.20   D. More than 700 games

The best spin to put on the early history of the Washington
Capitals might be that they had a long-term struggle for
respectability. But, in reality, they were *the* club to pillage
for points. The Caps' growing pains were considerable: lack-
lustre talent; dismal performances that set all-time league
lows in fewest wins and most losses; a parade of management changes that included the hiring of 26-year-old Gary
Green, the youngest coach in NHL history, and an eight-year
playoff jinx that dragged on for a record 720 games before
the Capitals' first playoff series in 1983. What broke the cycle
of mediocrity and ended Washington's postseason curse
was a crucial six-player trade with the Montreal Canadiens.
The franchise subsequently delivered its first .500 season in
1982–83 and first playoff spot, which concluded in a divisional
semifinal loss to the New York Islanders.

Plus-Minus Winners

IN 2005–06, **OTTAWA DEFENSEMAN** Andrej Meszaros
almost accomplished what no other NHLer has since plus-
minus totals became an official statistic in 1967–68. For much of
the season, Meszaros led all players in the plus-minus column as a
rookie. He slowed in the stretch, but still finished the season tied
for third with a plus-34, just one back of leaders Wade Redden and
Michal Rozsival at plus-35. Meszaros still has some distance to go to
catch Bobby Orr's record six plus-minus titles and plus-124, however.
Below, match the plus-minus leaders to their numbers and seasons.

Solutions are on page 122

PART 1

1. _____ Boston's Bobby Orr
2. _____ Detroit's Chris Chelios
3. _____ Montreal's Larry Robinson
4. _____ Edmonton's Wayne Gretzky
5. _____ St. Louis' Chris Pronger
6. _____ Pittsburgh's Mario Lemieux
7. _____ Calgary's Brad McCrimmon

A. Plus-55 in 1992–93
B. Plus-120 in 1976–77
C. Plus-98 in 1984–85
D. Plus-124 in 1970–71
E. Plus-48 in 1987–88
F. Plus-52 in 1999–2000
G. Plus-40 in 2001–02

PART 2

1. _____ Colorado's Peter Forsberg
2. _____ NYI's Bryan Trottier
3. _____ New Jersey's Scott Stevens
4. _____ Philadelphia's Mark Howe
5. _____ Tampa Bay's Martin St. Louis
6. _____ Boston's Bobby Orr
7. _____ Montreal's Brian Engblom

A. Plus-35 in 2003–04
B. Plus-63 in 1980–81
C. Plus-65 in 1968–69
D. Plus-85 in 1985–86
E. Plus-52 in 2002–03
F. Plus-53 in 1993–94
G. Plus-76 in 1978–79

7

The *H*ardest Act

WELCOME TO THE TOUGHEST TOURNAMENT in sports. After doing battle in the 2006 Stanley Cup finals, the Carolina Hurricanes and Edmonton Oilers became forever linked by a much less honourable distinction after each failed to qualify for the 2007 playoffs. In NHL history, Carolina and Edmonton are the only finalists to both miss postseason play the following year. Worse, the 'Canes joined only six other defending Cup champions, including the 1969–70 Montreal Canadiens and the 1995–96 New Jersey Devils, that stalled the next season. Sometimes the hardest act to follow is your own.

Answers are on page 108

7.1 **As of 2006–07, who has appeared in the most postseasons?**

A. Gordie Howe

B. Larry Robinson

C. Raymond Bourque

D. Chris Chelios

7.2 **How many games did Roberto Luongo play before experiencing his first playoff match?**

A. Less than 200 regular-season games

B. 200 to 300 regular-season games

C. 300 to 400 regular-season games

D. More than 400 regular-season games

7.3 What NHL first did Chris Pronger produce during the 2006 Stanley Cup finals?

A. The first shorthanded breakaway goal in finals history

B. The first penalty-shot goal in finals history

C. The first hat trick by a defenseman in finals history

D. The first game misconduct in finals history

7.4 What is the fewest number of total goals scored by a winning team in a playoff round?

A. One goal

B. Four goals

C. Six goals

D. Eight goals

7.5 Which team was the first to win the Stanley Cup without a captain?

A. The Detroit Red Wings in 1943

B. The Toronto Maple Leafs in 1962

C. The Boston Bruins in 1970

D. The Montreal Canadiens in 1986

7.6 The greatest single-game comeback in postseason history belongs to Los Angeles, who erased a record five-goal deficit against Edmonton in the so-called Miracle on Manchester in April 1982. What is the largest comeback (in goals scored) in Stanley Cup finals play?

A. Two goals

B. Three goals

C. Four goals

D. Five goals

7.7 Which coach is credited with first using regular line changes to win the Stanley Cup?

A. Lester Patrick of the Victoria Cougars

B. Eddie Powers of the Toronto St. Patricks

C. Leo Dandurand of the Montreal Canadiens

D. Percy Thompson of the Hamilton Tigers

7.8 Who owns the longest shutout streak by a rookie in the playoffs?

A. Detroit's Normie Smith in 1936

B. St. Louis's Brent Johnson in 2002

C. Anaheim's Jean-Sebastien Giguere in 2003

D. Anaheim's Ilya Bryzgalov in 2006

7.9 Which long-time NHL playoff record held by Maurice Richard did Joe Sakic break in 2006?

A. Most overtime goals in a career

B. Most overtime goals in one playoff year

C. Most overtime goals in one playoff series

D. All of the above

7.10 Which player in the 2006 playoffs joined hockey legends Newsy Lalonde and Maurice Richard as the only NHLers ever to score all four or more of his team's goals in a playoff game?

A. Joffrey Lupul of the Anaheim Mighty Ducks

B. Fernando Pisani of the Edmonton Oilers

C. Patrick Marleau of the San Jose Sharks

D. Rod Brind'Amour of the Carolina Hurricanes

7.11 What is the record for most points by a defenseman in a Stanley Cup finals game?

A. Four points

B. Five points

C. Six points

D. Seven points

7.12 Who is the youngest player ever to lead the Stanley Cup playoffs in scoring?

A. Montreal's Howie Morenz in 1924

B. Toronto's Andy Blair in 1929

C. Detroit's Gordie Howe in 1949

D. Carolina's Eric Staal in 2006

7.13 How many times in history has an NHLer had his name etched on the Stanley Cup without playing any games for his team during that championship season?

A. It has never happened

B. Only once: Vladimir Konstantinov with Detroit in 1998

C. On four occasions

D. More than five times

7.14 In the 2006 Stanley Cup playoffs, who scored the first overtime shorthanded goal in finals history?

A. Edmonton's Chris Pronger

B. Carolina's Rob Brind'Amour

C. Carolina's Eric Staal

D. Edmonton's Fernando Pisani

7.15 In what decade did the first on-ice awarding of the Stanley Cup take place?

A. In the 1920s

B. In the 1930s

C. In the 1940s

D. In the 1950s

7.16 In which city was the first Stanley Cup parade held?

A. Winnipeg

B. Toronto

C. Montreal

D. Ottawa

7.17 How many hours was the longest Stanley Cup parade?

A. Less than four hours

B. Between four and six hours

C. Between six and eight hours

D. More than eight hours

7.18 The smallest town to win the Stanley Cup celebrated the 100th anniversary of its championship in January 2007. Which town and team were the improbable Cup winners of 1907?

A. The Kenora Thistles from Ontario

B. The Winnipeg Victorias from Manitoba

C. The Renfrew Creamery Kings (Millionaires) from Ontario

D. The Dawson City Nuggets from the Yukon

Answers

7.1   D. Chris Chelios

In 23 NHL regular seasons, Chris Chelios has participated in the playoffs a near-perfect 22 times—eclipsing Raymond Bourque's previous record of 21. The only postseason without Chelios between 1984 and 2007 was in 1998, when his Chicago Blackhawks finished ninth in the Western Conference. And yet, while Chelios leads all greybeards in years, Gordie Howe is still the oldest player to compete in the playoffs. To match Howe, Chelios would have to play until he was 52, Howe's age in his last playoff game in 1980. But Chelios is likely to lead another playoff category as games-played leader. As of 2007, he was one game shy of Roy's 247, with 246. Chelios won Cups with Montreal in 1986 and Detroit in 2002.

7.2   D. More than 400 regular-season games

It took Roberto Luongo a league record 417 games to get a taste of postseason, but he made up for lost time in his first start on April 11, 2007. It might have been a case of "be careful what you wish for," except for the results. Luongo's Vancouver Canucks and Marty Turco's Dallas Stars battled through seven periods and 138-plus minutes of hockey before Henrik Sedin scored at 18:06 of the fourth overtime, the sixth-longest match in league history. The game dragged on for exactly five hours and 21 minutes, ending at 12:32 AM Pacific Daylight Time, with Bobby Lu facing a modern-day record of 76 shots and stopping 72 in the 5–4 Canucks win. "I got all the experience I needed in one game," Luongo said afterwards of the career-defining experience he categorized as the "most exhausted I've ever been." Among modern-era netminders, Luongo's herculean effort falls one short of Kelly Hrudey's 73 saves on April 18, 1987, but leads all debuts by rookies (including Jean-Sebastien Giguere's 63-save performance on April 2003) in this category since the NHL began compiling shots on goal in 1956. The all-time leader is Detroit's Normie Smith, who stopped all 90 shots in his first playoff game on March 24, 1936—the longest overtime in NHL history.

7.3 B. The first penalty-shot goal in finals history

Chris Pronger's historic goal on a penalty shot during Game 1 of the 2006 finals received little attention after the match. But at the time, it was seismic—giving Edmonton a 2–0 lead against Carolina at 10:36 of the second period. Pronger was awarded the penalty shot after referee Mick McGeough called Hurricanes defenseman Niclas Wallin for covering the puck in the crease. Edmonton coach Craig MacTavish chose Pronger, who lumbered in on Cam Ward and snapped a 14-foot riser past the Carolina goalie. It was the ninth penalty shot awarded in finals history. All previous shots were unsuccessful.

7.4 A. One goal

It's impossible for a team today to win a playoff series by scoring just one goal, but, prior to 1936, when early rounds were decided by total-goals format, it was doable. Under that format, teams with the highest goal count after two games won the series, and scoreless games ended in regulation. So what is the lowest goal total accumulated by a winning team? On two occasions, NHL clubs staved off playoff elimination by scoring just one goal. In 1929's quarterfinal subway series between New York's Americans and Rangers, neither team scored until the second overtime period in Game 2. The Rangers' Melville Keeling notched the series winner on Roy Worters, and, despite surrendering just one goal, the Americans were eliminated—with the Rangers winning the total-goals series 1–0. More dramatically, in 1935, the same one-goal total lifted the Montreal Maroons over the Chicago Blackhawks in quarterfinals action and took the team to the semis, where the Maroons' slim, 5–4 total-goals win against the Rangers earned them a Cup finals berth. The Maroons faced Toronto, the first-place team that had beaten them in five of six games during the regular season. But the Maroons were in the zone after two squeaker series and swept the Maple Leafs in three games in the best-of-five round. It was a Cup victory that began on Baldy Northcott's lone goal against Chicago in one of the last total-goals series in NHL history.

7.5 C. The Boston Bruins in 1970

Boston is the first, last and only NHL franchise to ice a Stanley Cup winner without a full captain. Between 1967–68 and 1972–73, the Bruins named no captain to their squad, including during the Cup-winning years of 1970 and 1972. There were four co-captains—Johnny Bucyk, Ed Westfall, Phil Esposito and the injured Ted Green—during the 1970 championship, but it was Bucyk who accepted the Cup from NHL president Clarence Campbell. When Boston repeated as champions in 1972, no Bruin wore the "C" above his heart. It was the last time a Cup winner was declared without a captain.

7.6 B. Three goals

The 2006 finals was a series about stunning comebacks. The most dramatic belonged to Edmonton, which clawed its way back from a 3–1 deficit in games against Carolina to force a do-or-die seventh match for the Cup. But the Hurricanes established the battleground with their comeback in the first game. Down by three Oilers goals, captain Rod Brind'Amour sparked the charge with a late second-period marker. In the third frame, Ray Whitney scored twice and Justin Williams added another on a shorthanded breakaway, giving Carolina its first lead of the game. Three minutes after Williams's goal, Alex Hemsky tied it 4–4. And then, the earth crumbled beneath the Oilers as playoff star and MVP contender Dwayne Roloson suffered a devastating series-ending injury, and little-used Ty Conklin took over and made a game-deciding blunder in the final minute after mixing up a routine play to team-mate Jason Smith. Brind'Amour then tucked the puck into an open net, handing Carolina a 1–0 series lead and the biggest comeback in finals history. (Five other teams have come from three goals down to win, including Pittsburgh in 1992 in a 5–4 victory against Chicago.)

7.7 A. Lester Patrick of the Victoria Cougars

Lester Patrick is one of hockey's immortals, whose contributions triggered major advancements in game play, organization and expansion of the sport. Throughout his hockey career as a player, coach, manager and owner, Patrick established numerous firsts, including a new strategy of line changes to beat the defending champion Montreal Canadiens during the 1925 finals. Patrick knew his aging team, though they had plenty of Cup experience, would be no match for the 60-minute men of Montreal, a team that had set endurance records the previous postseason by playing its regulars without substitution. So while most teams carried spares who rarely saw ice time, Patrick devised a novel strategy for his subs: frequent line changes every two to three minutes with the regulars. "Who could stop Morenz, Joliat and Boucher?" Patrick later said. "Who could score on the great Vezina? But I knew we'd win because our second line would just tire them out, and it did." Fatigue and frustration set in on the Montreal bench by Game 2, and the Canadiens managed just one win in the best-of-five series, with Victoria soundly defeating its eastern foe 3–1. Patrick's on-ice tactics had won the day, and the Cougars captured the Cup. The proud era of the 60-minute man was history.

7.8 D. Anaheim's Ilya Bryzgalov in 2006

George Hainsworth's legendary playoff shutout streak has had real estate in the NHL record books since he set down stakes with 270 minutes and eight seconds in 1930. Contenders such as old-time puckstoppers Dave Kerr (248:35) and Normie Smith (248:32) have taken their legitimate run, but, until Ilya Bryzgalov, no one in 75 years of playoff action has come as close to claiming hockey's greatest postseason shutout record. For that, Hainsworth can thank Colorado's Dan Hinote. Bryzgalov's streak began after Stephane Yelle scored Calgary's lone goal at 10:18 of the first period on May 1 and ended on Hinote's late first period goal at 19:33 on May 9, a shutout sequence of 249 minutes and 15 seconds. Bryzgalov fell agonizingly short of Hainsworth by 20:53, or roughly, a period of hockey. But the Russian rookie actually came much closer. After Hinote's goal, Bryzgalov held Colorado until Jim Dowd scored at 4:47 of the third period. Had Bryzgalov denied Hinote, he would have passed Hainsworth's record by more than four minutes, breaking the long-standing mark. As it is, Bryzgalov's 249:15 established a new rookie mark. Unfortunately, though the league recognizes scoring feats by rookies, it still does not acknowledge the accomplishments of freshmen goalies such as Bryzgalov.

Longest Shutout Sequence in One Playoff Year*

LENGTH	GOALIE	TEAM	DATES
270:08	George Hainsworth	Mtl	March 28 to April 3, 1930
249:15	Ilya Bryzgalov	Ana	May 1 to May 9, 2006
248:35	Dave Kerr	NYR	March 25 to April 6, 1937
248:32	Normie Smith	Det	March 24 to 28, 1936
218:42	Gerry McNeil	Mtl	March 27 to 31, 1951
217:54	J.S. Giguere	Ana	May 5 to 16, 2003

*Includes 2006–07

7.9 A. Most overtime goals in a career

When Maurice Richard retired, in 1960, he held an amazing eight of the 14 playoff records available to scorers. Almost 50 years later, however, his legendary collection has shrunk to include just a few shared marks, and his achievements as hockey's most dominant clutch performer have all but disappeared from the books. The last record Richard owned outright was finally broken by Joe Sakic, when the Colorado sniper scored his seventh career overtime goal against Dallas' Marty Turco on April 24, 2006. The goal ended the Rocket's 46-year reign as the all-time leader of six extra-period tallies. Sakic scored on a tip-in off a John-Michael Liles slap shot from the point at 4:36 of overtime in the 5–4 Colorado win. It was Sakic's 79th goal in 12 playoff seasons. Richard's career-high 82-playoff-goals record has long since been broken several times.

7.10 A. Joffrey Lupul of the Anaheim Mighty Ducks

Let's face it, Joffrey Lupul isn't likely to ever garner the kind of greatness bestowed on Hall of Famers Newsy Lalonde or Maurice Richard. Maybe, it's the name. Said forwards or backwards, "Lupul" just doesn't have a regal ring to it. Yet after the night of May 9, 2006, when he potted all four of Anaheim's goals in a 4–3 overtime win against Colorado, Lupul can lay claim to some fame because he duplicated only what Lalonde and Richard had managed previously: scoring all four, or more, of his team's goals in a single playoff contest. Lalonde recorded four goals in a 4–2 victory against Seattle on March 22, 1919; 25 years later, on March 23, 1944, Richard notched five tallies in a 5–1 match over Toronto. Lupul can also tuck in another little accolade for immortality's sake. He is the first player in playoff history to cap a four-goal night with an overtime score. After the match, Lupul said he hadn't scored four times in a game since junior hockey.

7.11 B. Five points

For his brief NHL tenure of just 26 regular-season games and 11 more in playoff action, little-known Eddie Bush managed to secure some prime space in the record books—most notably for his 43 years as the league's leader among defensemen, with five points in a playoff game. Paul Coffey's six-pointer changed all that in May 1985, but Bush still shares the lead in finals series play. Remarkably, among those half-dozen players are forwards Sid Abel, Toe Blake and Jari Kurri; Bush is the only rearguard. His date with destiny was April 9, 1942, when he scored one goal and four assists to figure in every Detroit goal of a 5–2 win against Toronto. It would be the last time the Red Wings won in the round. They took a commanding

3–0 series lead only to tank in the next four contests, handing the Maple Leafs the most incredible comeback in Stanley Cup history.

7.12   C. Detroit's Gordie Howe in 1949

One of the best stories from the 2006 playoffs was the stellar play of sophomore Eric Staal, who averaged better than a point per game to lead Carolina to the Stanley Cup. Stall scored 28 points in 25 playoff games to became one of only four 21-year-olds to lead all postseason scorers in the NHL annals—the youngest since Gordie Howe topped all point-earners in 1949 and the third youngest of all time. Howe was 21 years and 16 days old, followed closely by Toronto's Andy Blair at 21 years and 32 days, in 1929. Neither Howe nor Blair, however, won the Cup during their postseasons. Staal was 21 years and 233 days, and Howie Morenz was 21 years and 277 days in 1924. Incredibly, Howe is also the oldest playoff scoring leader, topping all shooters with 19 points in 1964. He was 36 years old.

7.13   D. More than five times

Vladimir Konstantinov is the most recent player to have his name etched in silver, despite being inactive during a championship season. Konstantinov was considered Detroit's spiritual leader in 1997–98, and the team's Cup win was a tribute to the Russian defenseman, whose career ended after a car accident the previous spring. In an emotional ceremony at centre ice, captain Steve Yzerman passed the Cup to the wheelchair-bound Konstantinov; the entire team then wheeled him around the rink in celebration. A few other teams have honoured inactive players with Cup inscriptions,

including the Montreal Canadiens, who recognized goalies
Richard Sevigny (1979) and Ernie Wakely (1965 and 1968), even
though they hadn't played a shift all year. (In Wakely's case,
he suited up in two career games for Montreal, one in 1962–63
and the other in 1968–69. His two championships for two
games' work must be the best Cups-per-game average by a
player on one team.) And in 1929, the Boston Bruins favoured
retired goalie Hal Winkler with Cup status despite the fact
that he was replaced in nets by Tiny Thompson the preced-
ing season. Then, the Bruins added the names Ted Green
and John Adams to the Cup's gleaming patina in 1970. Green
had been sidelined the entire season with a fractured skull,
and Adams was the Bruins' third goalie, a minor leaguer in
Oklahoma City who didn't see NHL action until 1972–73.

7.14 D. Edmonton's Fernando Pisani

Hometown hero Fernando Pisani scored a playoff-high five
game-winning goals during Edmonton's improbable 24-game
Cup run in 2006, but his most important game-winner came
in Game 5 against Carolina with his team down 3–1 in the
series. At 3:03 of overtime, Edmonton looked in deep trouble.
Moments earlier, the Hurricanes' Michael Peca rang a shot
off the post and Oilers defenseman Steve Staios was called
for tripping, giving Carolina the man-advantage and a huge
opportunity to win the game and claim the Cup. But Cory
Stillman's cross-ice breakout pass failed to reach Eric Staal,
when, moving in to disrupt the play, Pisani performed a little
miracle. "The puck was kind of going slow and I decided to go
for it. [Staal] has a long reach, and I got my stick on it as well.
It hit me in the chest, and all of a sudden I looked up and I've
got a breakaway on the goalie." Carolina goalie Cam Ward
cheated on his blocker side, so Pisani shot it in the top half of

the net, glove side. The breakaway goal was the first overtime shorthanded goal in finals history and the first of its kind to prevent a team from elimination. Final score: 4–3.

7.15 B. In the 1930s

Until the 1930s, it likely had never been done before: not on a baseball diamond, a basketball court, a football gridiron or a hockey ice surface. Championship trophy presentations were typically reserved for the locker room or black-tie banquets— until the NHL moved the ceremony on-ice during the 1930s. But by no means did the practice become a league-wide tradition (that wouldn't happen until the 1950s). It was sporadic at best, with newspaper reports of jubilant speeches by Conn Smythe and others at Maple Leafs Gardens in 1932. Then, two years later, immediately following Chicago's stunning victory over Detroit, NHL president Frank Calder presented the Cup to club owner Fred McLaughlin and his triumphant Blackhawks before a euphoric crowd at Chicago Stadium. The *Detroit News* reported that during the on-ice celebrations, Hawks winger Louis Trudel "grabbed the Stanley Cup as soon as it was brought on the ice for the presentation and skated wildly around the rink" (which takes the shine away from Ted Lindsay, who is recognized at the first player to pick up the Cup and carry it around the rink—after the Red Wings won in 1950). It wasn't until the 1980s that the other three major team sports adopted hockey's rink ritual and made the fans part of their year-end celebrations.

7.16 A. Winnipeg

Stanley Cup champions had been honoured with gifts, banquets and celebrations at their home rink, but the first Cup parade took place in Winnipeg in February 1896 for the hometown Victorias. After stunning the Montreal Victorias with a 2–0 winner-take-all victory at Montreal's Victoria Rink (yes, apparently everything was named after the great dame in the Victorian age), Winnipeg held many celebrations, including a parade on Main Street with the Stanley Cup travelling in one of the cabs. It was the first time a western club had won the Cup, and, upon its return by train from Montreal, the team had the locomotive's cow catcher festooned with hockey sticks and brooms to symbolize the Vic's clean sweep in Montreal. Cup parades, as we know them today, began in 1907 when the Montreal Wanderers received a long parade through Montreal streets that concluded at the famous Savoy Hotel.

7.17   D. More than eight hours

Montreal mayor Jean Drapeau had a knack for the spectacular. His world's fair to celebrate Canada's centennial, Expo 67, was a marvel that drew international praise and 50 million visitors to man-made islands in the St. Lawrence River. At the same time, he built an underground city that was connected by a sleek and innovative subway system. Drapeau also had a hand in landing a Major League Baseball franchise, and brought the 1976 Olympics Games to town. These accomplishments might have all been predicted, however, considering his grand plans to organize a Stanley Cup parade for the Canadiens in 1956. Drapeau's parade route took the team along 30 miles of Montreal streets, from the Montreal Forum through all 11 city districts, and finished at City Hall—a gruelling eight-hour, 30-minute route that was nearly twice as long as expected. Legendary coach Toe Blake was so furious, he threatened to never win another Cup if the mayor subjected his team to such celebrations again.

7.18 A. The Kenora Thistles from Ontario

When Kenora challenged the Montreal Wanderers for the Stanley Cup in January 1907, the playoff matchup was billed as "a battle between a small town and a big city, rough and raw Western Canada against the rich and refined East" by John Danakas and Rick Brignall in *Small Town Glory*. At the time, Montreal was Canada's most modern city, while Kenora was just a speck in the wilderness of northwestern Ontario. Still, the mining and lumber outpost boasted a Hudson's Bay fort, a Mounties police house and the Canadian Pacific Railway running through its heart, and its sports were as big as the outdoors—with lacrosse, baseball, rowing and sailing in the warm months and hockey the rest of the year. The game was played mostly on frozen creeks and rivers, but Kenora did have Victoria Rink, where the Thistles refined its fast-skating brand of play. The team iced five locals from town and two ringers, goalie Eddie Geroux and the famous Art Ross. (Two other players made the trip but did not play: Joe Hall and Russell Phillips.) And after two previous Cup losses (in 1903 and 1905), the club was skilled, road-tested and ready to take the Wanderers—even in front of Montreal crowds at Westmount Arena. The Thistles stunned the defending Cup champion Wanderers by stealing both games (4–2 and 8–6) in an improbable best-of-two total-goals series victory. Receiving the news via telegraph, euphoric Thistles fans celebrated on the small-town streets of Kenora. Their unforgettable championship was also honoured in January 2007 with minor hockey games, an exhibition match between Kenora players and NHL old-timers and a long-overdue visit by the Stanley Cup. Kenora remains the smallest town to win the Stanley Cup or any major sports championship, while the upstart Thistles are a lasting reminder of how the West was really won.

Solutions to Games

Game 1: Moments in Time

1. February 22, 1980: The Americans won Olympic gold
2. March 23, 1994: Wayne Gretzky scored number 802
3. June 27, 1972: Bobby Hull signed with the WHA
4. March 22, 1923: Foster Hewitt's first radio broadcast
5. September 28, 1972: Paul Henderson scored for Canada
6. November 1, 1959: Jacques Plante donned his mask
7. February 18, 1985: Scotty Bowman passed Dick Irvin's 690 wins
8. February 7, 1976: Darryl Sittler's scored his record 10-point game
9. March 18, 1945: Maurice Richard notched 50 goals in 50 games
10. December 31, 1988: Mario Lemieux scored five goals in every possible way in one game

Game 2: Lowering the Boom

PART 1
1. E. Chris Simon (25 games); Ryan Hollweg (March 2007)
2. A. Marty McSorley (23 games); Donald Brashear (February 2000)
3. F. Gordie Dwyer (23 games); Abusing officials and exiting the penalty box to fight (September 2000)
4. C. Dale Hunter (21 games); Pierre Turgeon (May 1993)
5. D. Todd Bertuzzi (20 games); Steve Moore (March 2004)
6. B. Tom Lysiak (20 games); Tripping an official (October 1983)

PART 2
1. D. Brad May (20 games); Steve Heinze (November 2000)
2. F. Eddie Shore (16 games); Ace Bailey (December 1933)
3. A. Maurice Richard (15 games); Striking an official (March 1955)
4. B. Wilf Paiement (15 games); Dennis Polonich (October 1978)
5. C. Dave Brown (15 games); Tomas Sandstrom (November 1987)
6. E. Tony Granato (15 games); Neil Wilkinson (February 1994)

Game 3: Not-Ready-for-Prime-Time Records

PART 1 (SKATERS)
1. Doug Smail recorded the most goals without a power-play goal in one season, notching 31 goals without a goal on the man-advantage in 1984–85.
2. Pavel Bure recorded the highest percentage of a team's total goals in

one season during the modern era. He scored 59 of Florida's 200 goals for a 29.5 per cent in 2000–01. Joe Malone owns the all-time mark at 42.9 per cent in 1919–20.

3. Tiger Williams scored the most goals by a penalty-minute leader in one season in 1980–81, when he notched 35 goals while leading the league with 343 minutes in box time.

4. Owen Nolen has the largest goal increase between two seasons with a minimum of 50 games. Between 1990–91 and 1991–92, he jumped 39 goals.

5. Tom Bladon recorded a plus-10 for the highest plus-minus in one game on December 11, 1977.

6. In 1990–91, Brett Hull had the largest goals-to-assists differential in one season on 86 goals and 45 assists—for a difference of league high of 41.

PART 2 (GOALIES)

1. Jacques Plante recorded the most consecutive games allowing two goals or less with 18 games with Montreal in 1959–60.

2. Terry Sawchuk amassed 44 victories with Detroit in 1950–51, the most wins by a rookie goalie in one season.

3. Ken McAuley gave up the most goals allowed in one season: 310 goals with the New York Rangers in 1943–44.

4. Michel Belhumeur recorded the most games without a win in one season: 35 games with Washington in 1974–75.

5. Bill Durnan lost only five times with Montreal in 1943–44, the fewest losses in one season, while playing in a minimum of 50 games.

6. Frank Brophy gave up a record 16 goals for the Quebec Bulldogs on March 3, 1920.

Game 4: Drafting Late

1. Cristobal Huet: Los Angeles (214th in 2001)
2. Marty Turco: Dallas (124th in 1994)
3. Pavel Datsyuk: Detroit (171st in 1998)
4. Michael Ryder: Montreal (216th in 1998)
5. Karlis Skrastins: Nashville (230th in 1998)
6. Henrik Zetterberg: Detroit (210th in 1999)
7. Tomas Kaberle: Toronto (204th in 1996)
8. Daniel Alfredsson: Ottawa (133rd in 1994)
9. Darcy Tucker: Montreal (151st in 1993)
10. Miikka Kiprusoff: San Jose (116th in 1994)
11. Eric Daze: Chicago (90th in 1993)
12. Nikolai Khabibulin: Winnipeg (204th in 1992)

Game 5: History Highlights

1. June 5, 1991: Brett Hull won the Hart Trophy and duplicated his father's MVP.
2. March 24 to 25, 1936: Mud Bruneteau ended the longest game in league history.
3. March 12, 1980: The Howes played together in the NHL for the first time.
4. March 17, 1955: The Richard Riot erupted in Montreal.
5. February 2, 1977: Ian Turnbull scored five times to set the record for most goals by a defenseman.
6. March 21, 1985: Bobby Carpenter scored the first 50th goal by an American.
7. December 8, 1987: Ron Hextall shot and scored the first goalie goal.
8. November 12, 1942: Boston's Bep Guidolin became the youngest NHLer, at age 16.
9. October 3, 1953: Jean Béliveau finally signed with Montreal.
10. February 24, 1982: Wayne Gretzky scored his 50th goal in his record-setting 39th game.

Game 6: Plus-Minus Winners

PART 1

1. D. Boston's Bobby Orr: Plus-124 in 1970–71
2. G. Detroit's Chris Chelios: Plus-40 in 2001–02
3. B. Montreal's Larry Robinson: Plus-120 in 1976–77
4. C. Edmonton's Wayne Gretzky: Plus-98 in 1984–85
5. F. St. Louis' Chris Pronger: Plus-52 in 1999–2000
6. A. Pittsburgh's Mario Lemieux: Plus-55 in 1992–93
7. E. Calgary's Brad McCrimmon: Plus-48 in 1987–88

PART 2

1. E. Colorado's Peter Forsberg: Plus-52 in 2002–03
2. G. NYI's Bryan Trottier: Plus-76 in 1978–79
3. F. New Jersey's Scott Stevens: Plus-53 in 1993–94
4. D. Philadelphia's Mark Howe: Plus-85 in 1985–86
5. A. Tampa Bay's Martin St. Louis: Plus-35 in 2003–04
6. C. Boston's Bobby Orr: Plus-65 in 1968–69
7. B. Montreal's Brian Engblom: Plus-63 in 1980–81

Acknowledgements

Thanks to the following publishers and organizations for the use of quoted and statistical material:

- *The Best of Hockey Night in Canada* (2003) by Stephen Cole, Canadian Broadcasting Corporation (CBC). Published by McArthur & Company.
- *Hockey: Canada's Royal Winter Game* (1899) by Arthur Farrell. Published by R. Corneil Print and made available digitally by Library and Archives Canada.
- *The Hockey News*, various excerpts. Reprinted with the permission of the *Hockey News*, a division of Transcontinental, Inc.
- *The Hockey Song* (1973) by Stompin' Tom Connors. Published by EMI Music Canada.
- The *National Post;* the *Montreal Gazette;* the *Globe and Mail;* the *Toronto Sun;* the *Detroit News;* the *Canadian Press;* the *Associated Press;* and numerous other books and publications that both guided and corroborated our research.
- *The Official NHL Guide and Record Book.* Published by Total Sports Canada.
- *Small Town Glory* (2007) by John Danakas and Rick Brignall. Published by James Lorimer and Company.
- *Total Hockey* (1998, 2000); and *Total NHL* (2003) by Dan Diamond and Associates, Inc. Published by Total Sports.

The author gratefully acknowledges all the help throughout the years from Jason Kay and everyone at *The Hockey News;* Gary Meagher and Benny Ercolani of the NHL; Phil Prichard and Craig Campbell at the Hockey Hall of Fame; the staff at the McLellan–Redpath Library at McGill University; Rob Sanders and Susan Rana at Greystone Books; designers Peter Cocking and Lisa Hemingway; Bruce Bennett and the photographers at Bruce Bennett Studios; the many hockey writers, broadcast journalists and media and Internet organizations who/that have made the game better through their own work; as well as statistical resources such as the Elias Sports Bureau, NHL.com, hockeyDB.com, CBC.com, eurosport.com, HHF.com and shrpsports.com; and inputter Joy Woodsworth and editor Anne Rose for their dedication, expertise and creativity. Finally, special thanks to Kerry Banks for all of his contributions along the way.